PRAISE FOR

THIS BOOK HAS BALLS

"We are dealing with an individual who tried to convince Willis Reed that Bill Russell was overrated. He is a sick man, and I often wonder what his life could have been like had the Knicks ever been a competent organization, but he has somehow managed to write a good book."

—Bill Burr

"Yes, Michael is actor. Yes, Michael loves the Knicks. Yes, Michael hated when I used to destroy Patrick Ewing. And yes, Michael is funny as hell. And yes, Michael knows more about the NBA than some of these NBA bums who are playing. And yes, this is a hell of a book."

—Shaquille O'Neal

"Michael is many things. He is a producer and actor and comedian, for starters. He is also crazy, passionate, funny, and intense. All of those qualities come through in his book. Along with a troubling fascination with hair pieces. All of it, of course, can be explained by his love for the Knicks, which even in good times isn't a remarkable experience. Buy his book and enjoy the ride."

—Colin Cowherd

1 2 3 4 5 6 7 8 9 10
FAIRFAX HIGH SCHOOL
11
12
7850 MELROSE AVE., LOS ANGELES, CA 90046
13
14
1985
1986
30 29 28 27 26 25
Fairfax
11
DETROIT

1560 EAST NEW YORK AVE.
WELCOME
TO
HOWARD HOUSES

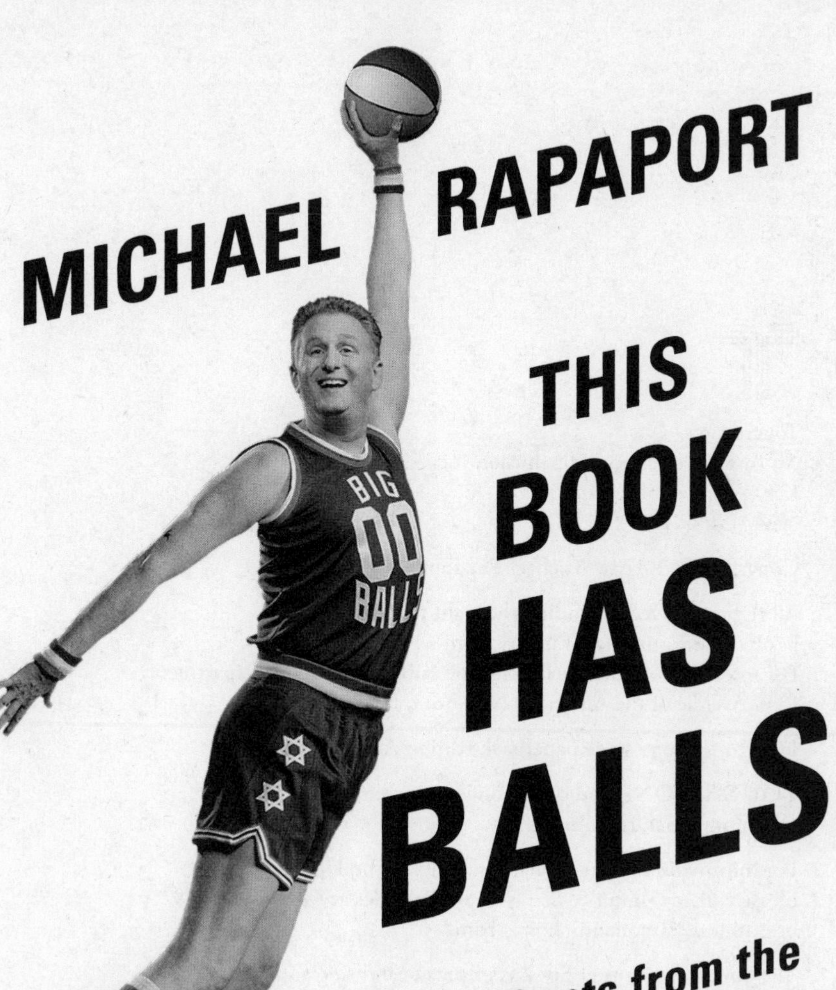

MICHAEL RAPAPORT

THIS BOOK HAS BALLS

Sports Rants from the MVP of Talking Trash

TOUCHSTONE

NEW YORK LONDON TORONTO SYDNEY NEW DELHI

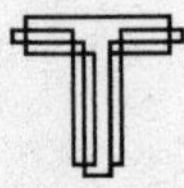

Touchstone
An Imprint of Simon & Schuster, Inc.
1230 Avenue of the Americas
New York, NY 10020

First Touchstone trade paperback edition August 2018

For information about special discounts for bulk purchases, please contact Simon & Schuster Special Sales at 1-866-506-1949 or business@simonandschuster.com.

The Simon & Schuster Speakers Bureau can bring authors to your live event. For more information or to book an event, contact the Simon & Schuster Speakers Bureau at 1-866-248-3049 or visit our website at www.simonspeakers.com.

Interior design by Kyle Kabel

Manufactured in the United States of America

10 9 8 7 6 5 4 3 2 1

Library of Congress Cataloging-in-Publication Data is available.

ISBN 978-1-5011-6031-8
ISBN 978-1-5011-6032-5 (pbk)
ISBN 978-1-5011-6033-2 (ebook)

Mom and Dad: Thank you for never squashing my dreams of being a professional athlete, although I'm sure you were well aware that it was far out of my reach from inception. I never think in limits because of you both.

Kebe: My love. Nobody would really understand or grasp how many snorts, smells, and quirks you put up with being my wife, best friend, and biggest supporter. You're everything to me, and I'm lucky to call you Wifey.

Hip-Hop: Anything I do, say, or create is inspired by hip-hop. I didn't talk much about you specifically in this book, but without you, hip-hop, and your influence on me, I'm just a plain-Jane cornball. Thank you for inspiring me, teaching me, and keeping me safe since 1979.

Contents

CONTENTS

An Imperative Note from the Editor

My first meeting with Michael Rapaport was offensive, disruptive, and honestly felt dangerous. He started telling me his thoughts about the book but then sneezed repeatedly and got up from the table without saying a word. He then came back a half hour later acting as if he had never left. I asked him what was wrong, and he told me he was allergic to my cologne and would I please leave immediately. I told him I didn't wear cologne, and he called me a liar and then he left the restaurant himself, leaving me both stunned and more than slightly concerned. I didn't know if I had just been fired, but apparently not, since Michael set up our next meeting at a local coffee shop. Within minutes of sitting down, Michael was tossed out and banned from the shop for insulting a guy who kept talking loudly with a British accent. Michael claimed the guy was faking the accent and there was no reason he had to talk that loud, then he threw a used napkin at him. I told him some people just speak that way, and then he shunned me and asked me to pay for his Uber home. I paid for the Uber, but when I received my Uber receipt, I realized he had taken an extra thirteen-mile trip to see a friend in Malibu. I was having serious doubts about whether we could work together.

Finally, I regrouped, and we met up at a new restaurant to work, and he seemed fine, but when I asked him about growing up in New York, he thought I was accusing him of lying about his upbringing and he left once again, this time leaving me with the entire bill. It wasn't until two weeks into the writing process that Michael and I actually sat down and got to work. By this time, we were getting along, but he had an issue with the chef at the place we were meeting. Michael said he was an anti-Semite because he kept sending out his toasted bagel cold. I told him it was an honest mistake, but Michael stormed out again, but not before yelling loudly into the kitchen something about the Nazi party. We were one chapter into the book at this time, so I was extremely worried. Finally, I figured it would be a much better working relationship if we did things through email and phone calls, and he agreed.

The first phone call did not go as planned. He said we were going to discuss his point of view on the new breed of basketball players, and by the time I had my notebook out, I heard sirens in the background and Michael was being told by the police that he had to stop letting his dog loose in the neighborhood without a leash or he would be placed under arrest. I knew then that this entire book would never get done if we tried the traditional writer/editor route of meeting, discussing, and reworking the material that I was used to. I had a volatile situation on my hands.

I tried calling his manager and couldn't get through for three days. When I got through, his manager told me this was "part of Michael's charm" and then he hung up the phone. I was beside myself for a month. Once again, we attempted to find a rhythm and actually dove into these chapters, and I felt we might be home free, until Michael told a waiter in skinny jeans that he had no business wearing that style of jeans, and if he brought him his soup wearing the same jeans, we were leaving without paying the bill. Again, the police were called.

I kept thinking to myself, how the hell does this respected working actor continue to thrive in society and function as an adult behaving this way? During one breakfast I asked him a question about his supposed athletic prowess on the court, and he took his shirt off in the middle of the restaurant and accused me of fat shaming. I'd never been through something like this before, but I'm a professional and love to challenge myself, so we met the following Monday at a well-known lunch spot in Hollywood.

When I got there, Michael was fighting with the manager because the manager had accused him of stealing panini sandwiches while standing in line. Michael said he planned to pay but was sick of waiting while Hollywood types took too long to order. The manager said he was three paninis in before he got to the register, and then ordered and never mentioned the paninis to the cashier. When I told Michael that it sounded like he was actually stealing, he left me at the restaurant alone and sent me an email telling me we would go back to communicating without seeing each other and chastised me for not using a proper facial cleaning astringent. He said my eyebrows were flaking and it disturb his thought process.

This kind of collaboration was certainly new to me, but we eventually found a system that worked for both of us. He would write alone and send me the material, then I would edit it and send it back, and he would complement me, offend me, and then hang up abruptly. This experience raised my already high blood pressure to a semi-dangerous level, but I realized that his disruptive behavior was part of his art and I had to adapt. I'd been working for too many years with professional adults and would have to readjust my style. I had to start thinking like a first-grade teacher trying to wrangle a class of unruly kids.

I must say I am incredibly proud of the end result. The book you are now holding captures Michael's point of view on a multitude of topics in a way that only he could. It's been anything but smooth sailing, and I've since been put on blood-pressure meds, but the end result I can live with. Michael offered to pay for my second executive physical at the Cleveland Clinic, which I took him up on, and I'm doing great. All my numbers are good, and I'm looking forward to my next assignment with preferably either a soft-spoken woman or a sedated man with human communication skills.

THIS
BOOK
HAS
BALLS

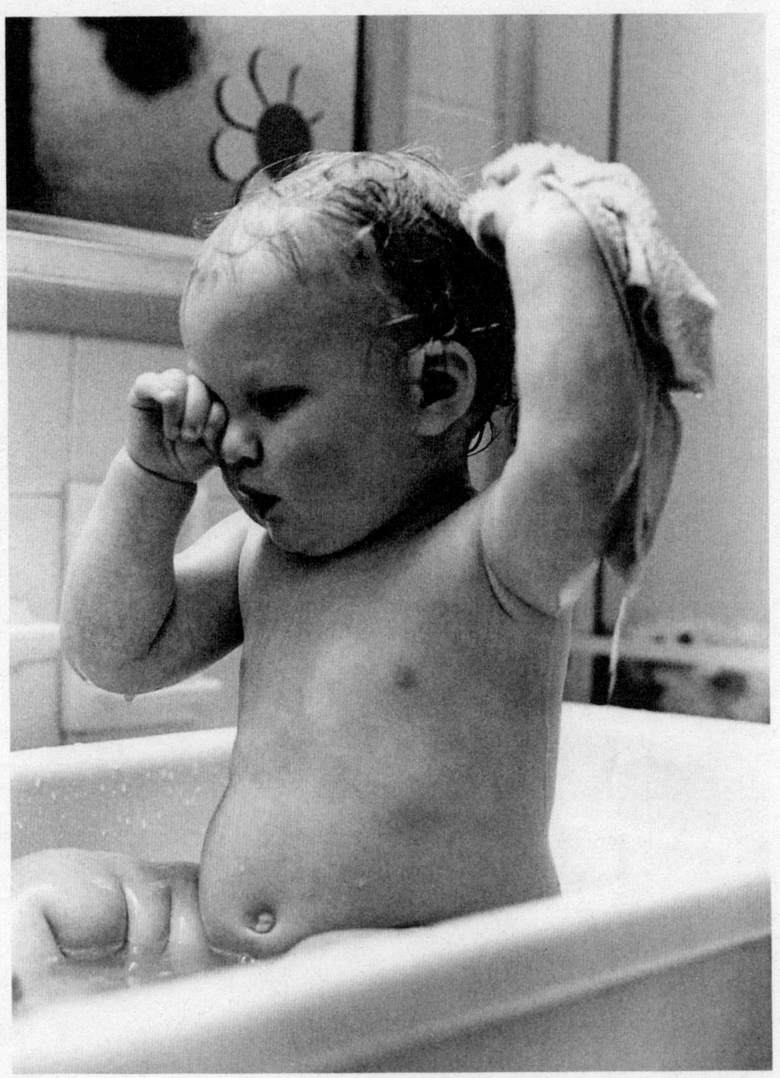

That's me in 1970. The calming bath before the storm.

Disruptive Behavior 101

Nine schools in twelve years. I was expelled or politely asked to leave nine schools in twelve years. That's some sort of record. Even in preschool, I was labeled disruptive and out of control. In fucking preschool. When I was four, they put me with the five-year-olds to reel me in after an incident involving looking up a teacher's skirt and knocking down a bookcase all in the same day.

That's a true story, and you can look up my records at Multimedia Preschool in Manhattan in 1974 if you don't buy it. For my first expulsion, I was kicked out of New York's PS 158 in the third grade for being belligerent, unruly, an overall pain in the ass, and shockingly unfocused. Getting kicked out of a New York City public school in the 1970s in the third grade was not an easy task. It took effort and drive. I wasn't just suspended, I was kicked out of the entire fucking school. One and done. When I think about it now, that's some real Rookie of the Year–type shit. Disruption was in my blood. I don't know how else to explain it. I was battling my DNA from jump street. DNA stood for Disruptive, Nuisance, Always.

There are no great stories of me beating up kids, setting fires, or flipping tables because it wasn't about that for me—although I did punch the principal during my last great stand when I was eight. Mr. Flanagan had a sad glass jaw. How an uncoordinated, flailing left hook from an eight-year-old gained so much attention I'll never know.

My mother would lovingly tell me, "Michael, you were born a pain in the ass." She was right. I was the king of the class clowns. I was a class clown on steroids, the Lance Armstrong of disruptive behavior and the Barry Bonds of ball breaking. You could say I was the Ben Johnson of pains in the ass. And it was all day every day, 24/7, for as long as I can remember.

Aside from being a Top Five Dead or Alive Ball Breaker, the only other thing that mattered to me at the time was sports. Playing sports was a part of my life as soon as I could walk. I played some sort of sport all day every day for as long as I can remember. It didn't matter what it was, I was down for any action. I loved it all. I played baseball, tackle football, and basketball. Starting at the age of six, I went to sleep-away camp for two months every summer and learned to play everything: tennis, soccer, track and field, archery, all of it. I couldn't get enough. I loved the competition. I loved the camaraderie. I loved winning, and I hated losing.

I would go through phases of wanting to be a professional football player after watching the Pittsburgh Steelers win games and seeing Lynn Swann make acrobatic catches. I'd want to be a pro baseball player because of Reggie Jackson's three-home-run World Series game, and even had a short spurt of wanting to be an NHL hockey player because of the 1979 New York Rangers, after watching Phil Esposito and Nick Fotiu fight. When I was ten years old I started going to a real boxing gym near Madison Square Garden because I decided I was going to be a pro fighter.

I would take the bus to the gym alone after school, train with a trainer, and then take the bus back home. When I imagined what

I was gonna do with my life when I grew up, I only imagined myself being a professional athlete. The sport changed, but the idea was to become a pro of some kind.

That all changed in the spring of 1979. Basketball kept resurfacing as my favorite sport. I loved playing it at the park and

Page two

The Timothy Dwight School

V and VI REPORT

NAME Michael Rapaport CLASS V DATE December 1980

SUBJECT	MARK	EFFORT MARK	COMMENTS
ART	D	4	Michael uses art periods to act out in an anti-social manner. He is very disruptive. S.C.
MUSIC	B-	2	Michael likes to sing and participate. He needs to tone down his energy level at times so that his participation can always be positive and not disruptive. J.L.
PHYSICAL EDUCATION	A-	1	K.S.
DRAMA	B	2	Michael is a very willing participant. He loves to perform but is not a good audience member. He sometimes lacks self-control. J.L.
ELECTIVE			
Homeroom Teacher's comments			Michael could be a productive and cooperative student. Unfortunately he sees school solely as a vehicle to play with his peers and badger his teachers. This is not conducive to social or intellectual growth and so he continues to flounder. J.G.
SCIENCE	C-	4	Michael needs to take his studies more seriously. He should strive to be more organized. He must take notes from class lectures and from the book. He also must pay more attention in class if he is to progress. J.M.

This is my fifth-grade report card. At this point I had attended four different schools. Shit was real.

at school. I played for hours with my friends and would shoot around alone for hours more. I was hooked.

Now, let's be real here—kids have access to every player on the planet these days. With video games, ESPN, and computers, kids literally know every player on every team by the time they're in the first grade. But back then I only knew about NBA stars like Kareem and Tiny Archibald and my New York Knick players like Walt "Clyde" Frazier and my main man, Earl "the Pearl" Monroe. I don't remember seeing them play that much, but we were always talking about them. My older brother, Eric, and I would play one on one, and I would be the Pearl and he would be Clyde and then we would switch off. I actually met the Pearl in 1980 at this diner in Manhattan on Seventy-Seventh Street and First Avenue called the Green Kitchen. My grandparents, father, brother, and I were walking into the diner and the Pearl was walking out, and I bumped right into him. I couldn't believe what I was seeing, and I said these exact words: "Earl the Pearl, give me some skin." The Pearl smiled, slapped me five, and said, "Have a good time." True story. The Pearl and Clyde were my guys until I found out about Doctor J, and then he became my new basketball obsession for real.

My first and only superhero, the Good Doctor Julius Erving. Doc was my idol. Even as a kid growing up in Manhattan, the Philadelphia 76er Doctor J was everything to me. I have no idea how I first found out about him or when I saw him play on TV, but he was it for me. I didn't give a shit about Superman, Batman, or even Bruce Lee at the time. Doctor J was all I cared about. And as much as I loved the Pearl, Clyde, and the Doc, my life took a dramatic turn as a nine-year-old when I watched Magic Johnson against Larry Bird in the NCAA Finals. That day my life goals changed forever. I was on a mission.

I was going to be in the NBA. That was it. I was going to be in the NBA and live my life accordingly and do whatever it took to make it to the League. There was no more flip-flopping sports anymore. I still loved and played baseball and football here and there, but now I was on a true mission to play pro basketball.

I watched Magic and Larry in that NCAA Finals game and saw every piece of TV coverage on both of them and went straight to the park with my basketball and started practicing. I lived a block away from John Jay Park on Seventy-Seventh Street and Cherokee Place on the Upper East Side. In the '70s, kids could go to the park alone and play all day, and parents didn't think twice about it. That's exactly what I did. All day every day I was there.

I remember seeing a clip of Bird making a baseline jump shot for Indiana State, and something about it resonated. So, I started practicing baseline jump shots over and over that day. I didn't move spots. It was all baseline all day. I was gonna be a pro basketball player, and this was where it was going to start. Fucking weird how kids' minds think. I told my mom and dad what I was going to do with the rest of my life and how they would reap the benefits. I was gonna buy them mansions and cars, and I was gonna do whatever I needed to do to play in the NBA. And the craziest shit was that, as much as I loved Magic Johnson—and, believe me, I loved Magic—seeing blond-headed Larry Bird play was what really sparked this dream for me.

Ironically, as soon as I saw him in a Celtics uniform, things were never the same for Larry and me. It wasn't like I grew up in a home that programmed me to hate all things Boston sports. God just blessed me that way.

My family, full of pure-bred New Yorkers, never taught me or influenced me to feel the disdain I felt for the Celtics, Patriots, and Red Sox growing up. I just took to it like a fish to water. Once again my DNA was taking over. As soon as the man who single-handedly influenced me to make one of the most important decisions of my life got drafted by the Boston Celtics, I couldn't stand him. I hated him as a Boston Celtic from day one. I was nine years old when Larry Joe Bird made his Celtic debut, and intuitively I found the whole thing repulsive. It's tough to express, but as I got older and started understanding the NBA better, somehow I hated Larry even more. It was like a virus that kept spreading. The green uniforms, that shithole arena they called the Boston Garden, I couldn't stand any of it. I detested it like a sickness. I never even took a moment to appreciate Bird's greatness as an NBA player. As a matter of fact, I wanna take a moment to publicly apologize to you, Larry Joe Bird. We didn't get off to a good start, and before I go any further, I would like to clear the air once and for all.

An Open Apology to Larry Legend

Dear Larry Bird,

You don't know me, but I know you. I once had a dream of being an NBA player, and at forty-seven years old I still have actual dreams of playing in the league. These are not like aspirations, my friend, these are real-life motherfucking dreams I have when I'm sleeping and shit. I actually had one a few nights ago that I was playing for the Seattle Supersonics during the Nineties, and Shawn Kemp and I were having an extensive conversation on the layup line about getting vasectomies. He got offended that I was bringing this up on the layup line, but I thought I was doing him a favor. Anyway, this isn't about the Reign Man, it's about us, Larry.

First, you are single-handedly my favorite white person with no lips. I mean that sincerely. I wanna tell you that even though I have spent a great portion of my life hating you as a basketball player, it was never personal. I'm here to admit that when I watched your Celtics play, I would refer to you as a Big-Nosed, Flat-Footed Fuck, and sometimes I'd even excitedly refer to you as a Mullet-Having Hillbilly Cocksucker. I didn't mean these things. I never did. I also didn't mean it when I would scream at the TV while watching you destroy my New York Knicks and kill my favorite adopted team from the Eighties, the Los Angeles Lakers. At that point, I was referring to you as "the No-Lip-Having, Non-Jumping Inbred Larry Fuck Face." I have no idea where I got those terrible ideas from, and I do now realize that words are powerful, Larry. And words can hurt. I get it, but I was young, and, Larry Bird, they were just words. I swear I did not mean what I was saying. After some real soul-searching, I realize today that it was your once-in-a-lifetime greatness I was screaming at. It was not your nose or even your lips. The funny thing was that as a twelve-year-old, I was actually nicknamed "Bird" by my friends, and to this day there's a bunch of people who still call me Bird when they see me. Isn't that funny, Larry Legend? I too had wavy blond hair, and to this day I still have a prominent nose. Most people would probably consider me a lot better looking than you, but who's counting? The point is, I got the nickname because I looked very similar to you, Larry Bird. Do you think I was just screaming at myself? Was I projecting my own frustrations for lacking foot speed and jumping ability and for having extremely pale skin onto you? Was I screaming at the fact that although we looked alike, I couldn't hit a jump shot to save my life? Was I just jealous of you because you were what I wanted to be and you made it look so easy, but for me it was impossible? Shit, Larry, shit!!!

I need to see a therapist about this, LB. You know any good ones? I'm gonna assume that you're not a psychotherapist kind of guy, so I'll just deal with this on my own.

Anyway, my personal Hoop Dreams were inspired by you, and although they became Hoop Nightmares by the time I was sixteen, I really wanna thank you for the inspiration and apologize for the loads of unwarranted hate I hurled at you during your playing career. It really wasn't personal. Of course, it did become a little personal in the Nineties when you were coaching and general managing the Indiana Pacers, but that's a whole other story that has no relevance here.

Nonetheless, Mr. Bird, I hope this letter finds you well in French Lick, Indiana, and I sincerely hope you consider accepting my apology.

Your Friend,

Michael "Bird" Rapaport

P.S.: Larry, this was me in 1983. I even secretly wore your T-shirt back in the day.

Ain't No Fact Checkin'

So, yeah, I didn't make it to the NFL, MLB, or NBA. I didn't even come close. I tried my best to become the best basketball player in the world. I literally practiced every day. I skipped Hebrew school, birthday parties, and family trips to play ball. I tried hard—maybe not hard enough—but it wasn't in the cards for me to be the Next Great White Hope in the NBA. Guys like my spirit animals Chris Mullin and Rex Chapman were the real deal. Some people may think I wasted a lot of time with a dream that went nowhere, but I have no regrets. I gained so much from it. My best friend to this day is a guy named Gerald, whom I met when I was twelve years old playing a pick-up game of three-on-three. Because of basketball I got to spend time in Harlem and the Brownsville section of Brooklyn. Being from the Upper East Side of Manhattan and having best friends in Harlem and Brownsville opened my eyes to a whole new world and a whole new perspective. In Brownsville, I was the only white kid who would come around and hang out. Gerald grew up in the Howard Projects, and I would go out there to play ball and would sleep over at his house after hours of playing. Going to Howard Park and seeing guys like World B. Free, Dwayne "Pearl" Washington, Jerry "Ice" Reynolds, and the Legendary James

"Fly" Williams play pick-up games right in front of me every day is something I wouldn't trade for anything. World B. Free is actually the person who gave me the nickname Bird in 1982. Being exposed to these people at such a young age was beautiful and shaped the way I see the world. Traveling on the subways of New York City to play in different leagues in random parks all over the five boroughs was a gift that I'll never take for granted. I don't regret any of the time I spent playing basketball in those days. It gave me real focus and strong goals in life. Unfortunately, basketball just wasn't what I was best at.

Yeah, I didn't make it to the NBA, but I can lift a five-pound weight and spin a ball at the same time. Can you?

At nineteen, when not a single college basketball opportunity presented itself and after a wild street fight left me with a quarter of my ear missing after it was bitten off by some maniac who didn't play by the basic street-fighting rules, I decided to officially shut down the "I'm gonna be an NBA player" phase of my life. It was over. The time had come to turn to something that had always came easier to me than playing sports: the fine art of breaking balls. I was good at it and I knew it. It was in my blood.

So, I moved to Los Angeles in June of 1989 with the goal of becoming a stand-up comedian. After years of honing my craft of antagonistic ball breaking throughout New York City, making people chuckle on stage wasn't that hard. I was a decent stand-up comic at best and I enjoyed doing it, but I finally found my calling when I first started acting in 1990. It came more naturally to me than anything I'd ever done in my life—

Wait a second, wait one single fucking second, hold the fuck on here. I need to stop this right now.

This book isn't the life and times of the world-renowned heartthrob and multifaceted thespian Michael Rapaport. This book isn't about my high cheekbones or drop-dead good looks that have left women breathless and men envious for the last twenty-five years. I'm sorry to disappoint you people, but this isn't about any of that bullshit. This book is about sports. So, let's reset.

I started off as a sports fan, and although the dream of playing pro may have died, I always remained a fan. Let's get clear about one thing first off the top: I don't talk stats and I don't talk data. I'm not gonna try to woo and wow you with all that yippity-yahoo, sugar-dicking statistical fancy-pants bullshit. Any hipster nerd sports geek with a computer can contrive some highfalutin statistics and tell you why one player is more important than another player. If you want stats, read the *Encyclopedia Britannica*. I don't do data. I didn't even stat-check my book until I was threatened with a lawsuit by my publishers.

What I like to do when it comes to sports is talk shit straight from my gut and let the chips fall where they may. This book is made up of my thoughts, opinions, rants, and heavy shit talking from the bottom of my heart, folks. It's rough, rugged, and raw dog without a bag. Can you dig it? I knew you could.

Going forward, you can read this puppy in order or out of order—it's all the same to me. You can read it in one magnificent and magical sitting, or you can take your time nice and slow and let it sink in. Jump around or read it backward, it doesn't matter. Just sit back and have a good time, because, ladies and gentlemen, this book has balls.

Why Lawrence Taylor Is the Greatest Football Player Ever

Lawrence Taylor is the greatest football player to ever play the game. Period. End of story. I don't even want to talk about this shit anymore. Yeah, I know Jim Brown ran over everyone in the world before he started acting in whacked-out action movies; I know all about Barry Sanders having the greatest footwork ever, rushing for fifteen thousand yards all while wearing that fucked-up helmet that was too big for his tiny head; and yeah, what I'm about to say kills me, but Tom Brady could be the greatest quarterback ever with his gelled-out Footlocker mannequin hair. There, I said it. But none of them can touch my man LT.

Lawrence Motherfucking Taylor was in a class all by himself.

You know why LT is the greatest of all time? Do I really need to spell it out? LT is the best of the best because for much of the time he was playing, he was on CRACK COCAINE!! One hundred eighty-two sacks! Ten Pro Bowls! It's never going to be duplicated. Four-time Defensive Player of the Year. And a regular user of that "Steal Your VCR Cuz I Have to Get High Again" shit. I'm not talking about performance-"enhancing" drugs here. I'm talking about performance-decreasing drugs. Crack is not what you want to be on while playing pro sports.

Do you have any idea how hard it is to play on crack? Ask Dwight Gooden! He loved the White Night Pipe, but he couldn't pitch on the shit. He couldn't even pitch after a night of heavy drinking. His system was sensitive. Not LT. He was a crack unicorn. If you think I'm exaggerating, then head on out to your nearest shithole neighborhood, find a fucked-up-looking building with someone outside wearing a winter coat in the summertime, buy a rock, smoke that shit, and run down the block. You're out of breath, right? Guess why? 'Cause you can't do shit on crack!

But Lawrence Taylor did. Yeah, he did. This degenerate superhero went to the strip club with mob bosses, fucked three hookers inside the club, drank a bunch of shit champagne with the rest of his fucked-up teammates, said good night, went to the stadium parking lot to sleep in his car before the game, woke up, hit the boulder, then went to the field, said "fuck the team meeting," and sacked everything in his path! That's a skill set you can't even train for. You can run sprints all day, spend your life in the weight room, learn the other team's offense, but guess what you can't do? Guess what's not in the training regimen when you get to the pros? Guess what's not in the playbook on day one of training camp? Playing on that Pure White Nose Candy! They don't teach that shit anywhere! They don't have you doing box jumps and crack hits. It doesn't work that way, okay? LT had a gift. He had more crack sacks than anyone in the history of the game ever. Let's take a little look here for fun. Here's how I imagine his true stats.

1981 NFL AP Defensive Player of the Year—On Crack!

1981 NFL AP Defensive Rookie of the Year—On Crack Nuggets!

1982 NFL AP Defensive Player of the Year—On Coke and Rum!

1986 NFL AP MVP—On tons of Coke and No Sleep!

1986 NFL PFWA MVP—On Hooker Woo-woo Coke Base Crack!

1986 NFL Bert Bell Award (Player of the Year)—On Purebred Ya-Yo Base Crack with No Sleep Again!

1986 NFL AP Defensive Player of the Year—On Flame-throwing Coke Flakes Bought from a Man in a Car!

Pro Football Hall of Fame First Team All-1980s Team—On Cuckoo for Cocoa Puffs Crack!

Pro Football Reference First Team All-1980s—On Hard Rock Blue Flake!

Yo, fuck playing through a little bit of shoulder pain! Don't cry to me about playing after your minor back surgery. Talk to me when you can fuck a prostitute, freebase for an hour, hit the pipe, and make First Team All NFL! Try one-hand collar tackling Ron Jaworski's fat white ass while you're hyped up on That Black Rock Boulder. Lawrence Taylor was in a class all by himself.

I know we can argue that Walter Payton could have been the greatest of all time, with lightning speed and who could throw the ball sixty yards, but give Walter that fucking Color Me Badd Coke Street Rock and a pipe and he's crying on the bench looking in the stands for his mother, who may or may not be there. Let's see Joe Montana hit some Purple Caps before a game, and guess what he's not doing? Passing for 4,500-plus yards again! No, he's not. He's hanging out by the San Francisco wharf looking for a transvestite and cotton candy! Let me see Tom Brady smoke that Snow White and the Seven Dwarfs shit in the streets and throw for thirty-six touchdowns again. Go ahead, Tom, smoke that Iranian Vagina and see what happens. You can't, man. You ain't LT. None of you are. Sorry.

One of my favorite comedians of all time was Richard Pryor. Pryor used to have this bit where the pipe talked to him. He would say the freebase pipe was calling to him, "Hey, Rich, I'm right over here if you need me, don't forget." And then Richard would argue back and forth with the pipe, trying to get the pipe to leave him alone. I can only imagine the relationship LT had with his crack pipe.

Pipe: Great game, man. Shit, I'm tired. You?

LT: Nah, I'm really not that tired.

Pipe: For real?

LT: Yeah. I'm pretty awake. Come here.

Pipe: Give me a minute, man. Chasing Aikman around didn't wear you out?

LT: I'll do that in my sleep. Motherfucker's flat-footed. We're going out.

Pipe: Like now?

LT: Yeah, now. My boys got that strip club on the Upper East Side. It's gonna be fun. Trust me. All the fellas are going.

Pipe: You sure you want me to go? I can stay home. HBO's showing the Roberto Duran fight tonight. I'll sit right here on the table and chill.

LT: I'm not going without you. No way.

Pipe: I don't want to cramp your style.

LT: My style? Everyone knows you. If you don't show, they'll ask where you are.

Pipe: Shit. I just wanted one night of rest.

LT: Rest is for pussies.

Pipe: Man, I don't know how you do it.

LT: I'm gonna grab a change of clothes in case we stay the night.

Pipe: Damn. Grab some water, then.

LT: Fuck water.

Pipe: All right.

LT: Next week we play Detroit.

Pipe: Detroit?

LT: Yeah.

Pipe: With Gary Danielson?

LT: Yeah.

Pipe: Shit, I could probably win that game on my own.

LT: Quit talking so much and let's go.

Pipe: Fuck it. Fill me up.

Listen, I don't really like that LT was battling drug addiction. It's not a joke. But I'm no rehab specialist and I don't judge. My point is, I really do think Lawrence Taylor was the greatest football player to ever play the game. He operated on a level very few athletes ever get to. And he had that thing, that X factor that doesn't come from being the fastest, it doesn't come from being the strongest or the smartest on the team. It comes from some other fucking stratospheric, god-given, way-out-there foreign place. I don't know. Ask Neil deGrasse Tyson. Whatever it is, Lawrence Taylor had it. And it sure as hell didn't come from the crack he was smoking, and I'm glad he's staying out of trouble these days.

An Open Letter to Tiger Woods

Dear Mr. Woods,

Can I just call you Tiger? This letter from me to you is in your best interest, trust me. Consider it to come from the people who love and admire you and have followed your career for many years. This letter is coming from a place of genuine love and concern. It troubles me that you were arrested for a DUI, and this time they said it was pills and not alcohol. I don't like to hear things like that. Sleeping in your car on the side of the road during a holiday weekend is not something to scoff at and should be looked into heavily. I also noticed things generally go bad for you over holiday weekends. I would find a way to stay home and relax during Memorial Day, Labor Day, Christmas, or Summer Solstice, for that matter. Just chill out when you see a holiday coming. You're obviously not fit for long weekends. Things can get better for you, though, Tiger, because people still care about you and would love to see you on the comeback trail. All that being said, I truly don't give a shit about golf. I never liked it and I struggle to come to grips with it when I hear it referred to as a sport. I think it's just a highly skilled game, and I would be fine if they never showed it again on television. But this letter has nothing to do with golf, my friend. It has to do with you. It has to do with your well-being and what I think might be the answer to your prayers.

This is a letter to a man who has lost sight of what got him to the mountaintop. I write it on behalf of the men, women, and children who have admired your work for so many years. We want to see you get back to being the BEST you that you can be. The great Tiger we know and love. The young man who won over the hearts and minds of fans all over the world. Yes, it's time to get back to doing what you do best. Eldrick Tont Woods, it is time to unfold the loaf, put it back on the streets, and FUCK your way back to the Masters!

Get back to that Grade A, Grade B, and—as we've all seen in the past and looked on stunned—Grade C Ass that made you the king! As soon as you took that loaf off the streets, your back went out, your game fell off, Nike said good-bye, and your game went into the shitter. You quit side pussy, and golf quit you. There's still time. It wasn't as if you were a bad person, Eldrick.

You weren't Pete Rose, gambling and drinking on camera. You weren't Aaron Hernandez in a gang war, RIP. You were simply dropping your pants all over America's wonderful landscape, because you weren't happy at home! I say break out the fucking black book and let the Hooters staff know that Eldrick Woods is back for some chicken tenders and a side of fat country ass!

Some players were better on steroids, some were better on speed, and you were the greatest golfer on planet Earth while tapping mediocre Midwest snapper. At this point, Mr. Woods, you're only hurting yourself by playing the good-guy role. So, get out of the house, call up Applebee's and Perkins twenty-four-hour joints, and tell that chubby divorced mother of three, "I'm sorry about the hiatus, but the Tiger is back and he wants his pole smoked in public and thanks for the extra side of bacon!" You deserve it. You changed the landscape of that shit game of golf!

When you were on that "late night let's fuck standing up" shit, you won four Masters. When you had that "Put it in your mouth while I'm eating a quesadilla"–type shit, you won three US Opens. But on your "Say No to Strange Campaign" you shit the bed. This is not how you go out. The men and women of this great country support you and want to see you back on top. We know you're a fuckin' animal, Tiger, and everyone accepts it. You hear me? You won fourteen majors all while your loaf was in the hands of strangers! It was beautiful to witness. PGA Player of the Year eleven times while that porn star had your balls in her mouth. The writing is on the wall!

Listen, I'm sure it wasn't great having the world learn you were that balls-to-the-wall buck-wild. I'm sure it felt weird having that much loaf exposure all at once. But you won championships when it was out, you lost when it was in, and, all in all, you did it your way. The Black Sinatra strikes again. Now let's get back to winning with that style you made your own.

You didn't do it Hollywood style either. This wasn't some "Have my agent call Scarlett Johansson and meet me at the Four Seasons" shit. You weren't clipping a Victoria's Secret model on the roof of the Ritz. You kept it grimy like an American Icon should. Was calling yourself Cablinasian some dumb shit and something I'm sure you regret? Yes. But you were fucked up in the head, and it could have been handled better. They should have sent Jim Brown to save you, but you weren't on his radar. He would have straightened you out in one sit-down.

Sponsors started dropping you like a bad habit. I know it sucked. But guess what, Tiger? Fuck Nike and Coke. You know how much Trojan would pay you for *not* wearing a condom? Get out there and do a Trojan commercial. Look dead-ass into the camera and tell the world, "I keep a Trojan in my pocket, and that's where it stays!"

Your Gatorade commercials were awesome, but you don't need that shit anymore. That shit gives people stomachaches and dehydrates them. You need to do a Schlitz Malt Liquor commercial and demand a percentage of the company, because you'll boost sales with ads like this: "When your wife smashes your windshield with your favorite golf club after suspecting you of cheating, the best way to forget this ever happened is to sip an ice-cold forty of Schlitz Malt Liquor and call your homies to vent." You'll break the bank with that one, Tiger.

I understand fame has its drawbacks. I get it. I see it every day, man. People lose it. It's a tough racket. So the fuck what? You weren't on heavy drugs, you weren't homeless with the bottle. You fell for some rug monkey, and that's it. Powerful men of industry have seen the kingdom crumble from the Pink Palace for years. Entire corporations have gone broke from one great piece of snapper. We get it, and we got you.

You need a harem of beautiful women at every hole waiting for you with water, sunblock, and a massage chair. Show up to the Masters in a pimp hat, bellbottoms, and six fine Brazilians on loan from Leonardo DiCaprio's pool! And bring a barber, too. Get yourself tightened up out there with some nice side clippers. No more lames in your entourage either.

You get yourself a real crew you can trust, not some frat boy who ratted you out cuz he didn't like you cheating. Fuck that. It's none of his business. You get some real road dogs. The way real players used to do it. You get one to wrangle, one to hold the money, and one for protection. That's what a real crew does. And get a cool celeb in your mix, too: fuck Michael Jordan. He's just going to try to take your fall-off chicks. Most people want to be like Mike, but he wants to be like you, Tiger. You don't need him. Get a crew with some flavor and credibility. Call Snoop Dogg. You and Snoop get some beautiful apple ass ready to quit the day shift at Denny's and win back what's rightfully yours! And ours! The game needs you, man. The people need you. Come back, Tiger. Call me, man. Seriously. Get back to your old self again. I can help you out.

My Gold Medal Sweetheart, Mary Lou Retton

When I think of the 1984 Olympics, the first and most important thing that comes to mind is Mary Lou Retton. I'm not exactly sure what happened with me and Mary Lou, but in the summer of 1984, I fell head over heels in love with her. This is totally strange, but totally true. This shit was real. When I say "fell in love," I'm talking about that "Show off in front of my girl, bring her fresh flowers, and make her father like me" type of love. I fell for real.

Yes, I watched Michael Jordan and Team USA win gold. I watched Carl Lewis do his thing. And I even remember Greg Louganis doing his dives. But none of them held a candle to my sweet Mary Lou.

As soon as she walked out onto the mat with those thick little baby feet, lightning struck. Maybe it was her smile, maybe it was her bubbly personality, or maybe it was her amazing apple-shaped booty. At fourteen I didn't realize I was a butt man, but it turns out I was. I was smitten, Mary Lou. I started planning our summer together, when I would bring you back to New York City to meet the family. I saw it all happening like I had a crystal ball.

She would come to the seven Bar Mitzvahs I was invited to, and everyone would love her just like I did, laughing and dancing and asking her to help hoist the parents in the chair because they knew she had strength and a great low center of gravity. And then on Sundays she would come to the park with me while I practiced free throws and she ate Mr. Softee ice cream and twirled around on the jungle gym waiting for me. You see what was going on here, right? I had entire conversations with her in my head.

Me: Hey, Mary Lou, hope you had fun at my dad's place over the weekend.

Mary Lou: Of course I did. He was so cool, and I love the long walks you took me on in the city. I never get to rest like that.

Me: You need me to rub your feet?

Mary Lou: Why?

Me: You said you never rest, so I figure your feet might be sore. I have strong hands, if you didn't notice.

Mary Lou: Thanks, Michael, but we have professionals who do that.

Me: I'll kill them.

Mary Lou: Huh?

Me: Oh, nothing. I meant, that's great.

Mary Lou: Yeah, it feels amazing.

Me: They're stupid.

Mary Lou: Why would you say that?

Me: I love you.

Mary Lou: What?

Me: What?

Mary Lou: Um, I have to get back to the hotel. They're honoring me tonight for my medals.

Me: Should I come? I could be there by seven, as long as I'm home by nine.

Mary Lou: Will your parents let you?

Me: Well, I'll have to ask my mother. Or maybe my brother can drop me off, but I'm sure it won't be a problem.

Mary Lou: Sure, I guess.

Me: Great. Then we can go to Nathan's for a dog and a Coca-Cola.

Mary Lou: Sorry, Michael, I don't drink soda.

Me: Fuck!

Mary Lou: Language, Michael!

Me: Sorry, Mary Lou.

I was so fucked up, I played out our married life, too. I was the comfortable husband, and she was the breadwinner.

Married Me: I'm starving, baby.

Mary Lou: I'll make some chicken pot pie.

Married Me: Yo, Wheaties called, you've got a photo shoot tomorrow at six a.m. Do the whole thing in a leotard, babe.

Mary Lou: Okay. What are you going to do all day?

Married Me: My boys are coming over to watch the Knicks game.

Mary Lou: Don't they work?

Married Me: Huh?

I'm telling you, it wasn't right. I was obsessed. This wasn't healthy. I'm still confused as to how or why this happened, but she became my primary focus during the summer of '84.

I was cheering her on for the few days she competed for the gold. And I knew nothing about gymnastics. I couldn't tell the difference between a backflip and a cartwheel. But I watched

Mary Lou compete for the All-Around, and when she landed her pressure-filled perfect 10 to win the gold, I thought I had won, too. I was in my sister's room and jumped up when she stuck her perfect landing, and I was jealous when Coach Béla Károlyi hugged her and carried her off the mat. "Put down my girl, you fuckin' weirdo."

My love for Mary Lou Retton was real. It was unshakable, and it wasn't going away anytime soon. After she won the gold I would follow all her TV appearances and interviews. I was in front of the TV doing full-blown Mary Lou Retton searches. I was changing channels all night like Rain Man waiting on Judge Wapner. Those were also the days of *TV Guide* magazine, where you could skim through and see who was on every night. I was speed-reading for the first time in my life, just looking for the word *Mary*.

I saw her on Johnny Carson, and I laughed when Johnny laughed when she was funny, but I also laughed when nobody laughed because I felt like I knew and understood Mary Lou Retton better than everyone else in the viewing audience. I would never let my apple-bottom bunny fall flat on national TV. Then I asked my dad to buy me the Wheaties box with Mary Lou on the cover, and he did. I really ate the damn cereal, too, because I was sure Mary Lou did. No way would my honest, sweet Mary Lou represent a brand she wasn't truly into. I just knew she was up every morning before practice in her PJs eating Wheaties. Well, guess what? So was I.

I kept one box in my closet next to my collection of *Sports Illustrateds*. I even bought an extra copy of the *SI* with Mary Lou on the cover that read, "Only You, Mary Lou." I needed an extra copy because I Scotch taped a mini shrine of my angel over my bed. True story.

This is the shrine to my sweet Mary Lou that hung above my head in 1984.

My friends would come over and be like, "What the fuck, man? Why do you have Mary Lou Retton shit on your walls?" I would make up excuses about it being for a class project or that my brother, Eric, put it up. I always felt ashamed that I didn't just own up to it and say, "I love Mary Lou Retton, and you motherfuckers just don't know what true love is yet, so when you find someone you truly love, you'll know what all this is about. Now get the fuck out of here." But I never said any of that. I was confused and filled with overwhelming man feelings. I didn't know what the hell was happening in my heart.

I was out of my mind. I really thought that somehow Mary Lou Retton and I were gonna meet, she was gonna be my girlfriend, and I would be the supportive boyfriend who would carry her gym bags. I was ready to go three bags deep on both shoulders like a lost father traveling with his family in the airport. I didn't care. Then we would be married and move back to her hometown of West Virginia, where I'd go to college, emerge as a great basketball player, make the NBA, finally let her rest her sweet puffy feet, and we would live happily ever after . . . I was fucking gone! And it didn't stop there!

The 1984 Olympic team had a traveling exhibition that made its way to Madison Square Garden. And I knew I would die if I didn't go there and meet her. I asked my father to get me a ticket, just one ticket. I'd have to go alone to meet Mary Lou to begin our life together. I remember my dad asking me, "What the fuck do you wanna see gymnastics for?" I honestly can't remember what I said, but I told him that if he got me one ticket to the event, it would be my Christmas present. We only did Christmas presents in my home, even though we were Jewish. I don't know, as a kid, the Christmas tree was just more fun. He got me the ticket, and it was game on.

The event was on a Saturday afternoon. I got up early and picked out my outfit: a white turtleneck shirt, a pair of burgundy Levi's, my "WhiteMike" nameplate belt buckle, and a gold Cuban link bracelet that I borrowed from my friend Randy. Of course, I also had on my Polo cologne. I sprayed that shit in the air, did the walk-through, then hit the neck and the shoulder area in case the hug from Mary got tight.

I got to the Garden extra early and tried to settle into my seat. I had to dab out my neck sweat from being in a turtleneck. It was a lot for a fourteen-year-old kid to be draped in. I remember being in my seat, looking around and seeing parents with young girls and some with boys who also loved Mary Lou Retton. (But not the way I did, of course.) There was every demographic there except mine: a lonely fourteen-year-old boy dressed like a displaced member of the Rock Steady Crew. I really had no business being there.

Before the exhibition started, the announcer invited the crowd down to the mats to watch the gymnasts warm up and do flips.

I stood up, adjusted my nameplate belt, and followed the crowd down. This was my chance. This was my moment, and I was not gonna miss out. I found my spot and posted up like that cool-ass kid playing the wall at the party. I stood along the mats on the floor of MSG surrounded by a bunch of little kids who were screaming and yelling and oohing and ahhing at every flip the gymnasts did. I was like, "Chill out, cornballs, you're fucking up my concentration." I was trying to focus. Where was my girl? Where was my Mary Lou?

And then I saw her. She stepped out of the tunnel like a tiny lone wolf: brave, strong, bowl-cutted out, and smiling, teeth looking extra white and perfect. She turned to wave to the other side of the arena, and the Garden went ape shit. Everyone was screaming and yelling her name.

Sweet Mary Lou walked the perimeter of the mat, touching the kids with only her delicate fingertips and waving hello to everyone. I remember thinking that she must be freaked out by all these screaming kids. And then my young life went into slow motion. Mary Lou Retton was coming over to my side. My heart was racing, my palms were sweating, but my hair gel was holding. She was twenty feet away, and we made eye contact. The only words I could get out were, "I love you, Mary Lou. Me and you, Mary Lou!" This was not planned. What the fuck? It just came out of me, and I know for sure she heard me because the eye contact stopped immediately and she looked away to her brother Ronnie or Donnie, whom I recognized from her *People* magazine spread but who didn't make it onto my wall cuz I trimmed him out. She said to him, "That guy looks weird." I literally saw her say that with my own eyes. I was crushed. I was humiliated, but she was right. I looked fucking crazy. She had every right to be concerned.

I had to go back to my seat to process what had just happened.

Why didn't she come over to me, hug me, and take me on the mat like I'd planned? I had to talk myself through this. "Michael, did you really just scream 'Me and you, Mary Lou'? Fuck, man." I knew it was over. I had really wanted things to go a different way for us.

I left early and walked all the way home. I was ready to rip down my mini shrine to Mary Lou, but decided instead to take it off gently and keep it in my magazine collection just in case we reconnected. I replaced her shrine with the Kurtis Blow mini poster my dad got me. I never felt the same for her again. I was heartbroken, but I had to move on.

I wound up giving my "WhiteMike" belt buckle to my first *real* girlfriend, Elsie from Wagner Junior High School. To this day, I have never met Mary Lou Retton again, so if you're out there, holler at your boy.

Good Men in Bad Pieces

What the fuck are they doing to my broadcasters? The gods of the play-by-play and kings of color commentary are being shamed before our eyes. These men are our national treasures. I'm talking about Al Michaels, Marv Albert, Dick Stockton, and my man Hubie Brown, just to name a few. These are the greatest broadcasters ever to get behind the microphone, and they're WEARING FUCKING WIGS on TV? Mike the Czar Fratello, I'm throwing you in there, too. Your hairpiece is off-center and wrong. The point is simple: These men should be free to be wigless and bald! Let the rug go! Toss them in the garbage and let your lumped-up heads shine bright. You're too good for this shit.

These men narrated every amazing sports moment in the last fifty years, and this is how you treat them? Every incredible moment you remember from the hardwood, the turf, or the diamond, these wordsmiths have called for you. When Dick Stockton called the 1975 World Series, you think he ever thought he'd be forced to put a spider monkey on his head? You think after calling Carlton Fisk's home run for the Red Sox he was envisioning himself with a bird's nest attached to his skull? Hell, no.

Al Michaels called the Miracle on Ice, one of the greatest

events in American history, and now you're forcing him to lay a rug down because you want us to think he's not losing hair? Let me repeat that: he called the Miracle on Ice! "Do you believe in miracles?" When I see the goalie Jim Craig looking for his father in the stands, I still cry on the spot. Big Al, live the life you want to live. You're a great man in a bad piece!

I know Marv Albert bit a hooker in '97, but that doesn't mean you need to shame him with a forced mop top that leans left and looks like it was ripped off a twelve-year-old boy's head. This is the man who gave us "Yes! Serving up the facial" when Kobe dunked on Yao Ming. Marv Albert is a goddamn diamond, a one-of-a-kind Jewish diamond. I'll tell you something, Marv, sports fans couldn't give two shits about the hooker incident. We're sports fans, not parole officers. We fucking love you, Marv, and we loved you even more after the hooker incident. It made you human. Who among us hasn't had a regrettable hooker incident? But we can't overlook the wig, man. You deserve better. I'm not offering a solution because I don't have one, Marv. I don't know psychologically where your head is at with this. I don't know what you're seeing when you look in the mirror, but I can tell you what we're seeing. We're seeing a legend of the game embarrassed on national television, forced to wear the hair of a young Brad Pitt. You deserve better.

Maybe this is all Howard Cosell's fault. I don't know. Maybe he started it all by wearing the first toup that was made for someone else's head. Howard, I loved you, but you started something that can't be reversed. Of course, most men struggle with some sort of hair issue later in life, and if you're not Bruce Willis, Michael Jordan, or my man from *The Shield*, a shaved head may not be for you. I mean, could you imagine Hubie Brown with a shaved head? Nobody wants to see that. But what the hell have they done to Hubie? I'm not saying we need him bald. I don't want to see it and his family and friends don't want to see it, but, Hubie, what the fuck is going on? You look like Billy Idol fucked Ellen DeGeneres! It doesn't make sense. You look like you stole that bad boy from the set of *Spartacus*. Your shit is old and young at the same time. Come on, Hubie!

I know damn well these icons are having the same thoughts, but they can't bring it up 'cause it's in their contract to never bring up wigs. I get the whole Hollywood "You have to look young on TV" of it all, but guess what, fellas? We were never watching you for your jawlines and great skin. We love you for your wordplay and game calling! Damn it. What really gets me is that we know this is not your doing! There's a Wig Conspiracy out there! The powers that be are forcing this on you. They're coming into your dreams and whispering shit like, "Hey, man, you're much better-looking with gray cadaver pubic hair on your head."

And Quick Dick Stockton, you're my man for real. I've loved you since the early Eighties, listening to you call all the CBS Sunday afternoon games. You walked me and the rest of the sports world through the highs and lows of so many great moments with that Golden Baritone voice. The fucking Barry White of the sports world. I love and appreciate you and your work. It's amazing that you're still calling games and your voice still sounds fantastic. Hearing you call an NBA game is like listening to Marvin Gaye while getting a foot massage. You're great, Dick. You're smooth. There is no one in the game who sounds like you, but you look fucking nuts! You look homeless and scared.

It doesn't even matter that you're wearing a suit to your job at this point because no one sees it—they're too busy questioning your head. It might look better if you dressed in a robe like Rodney

Dangerfield. Dick, please hear me out here. I used to see Rodney Dangerfield walking around my neighborhood on the Upper East Side in pajamas, a robe, and slippers in broad daylight. It was like he went out to get the paper and just kept walking. He would be rolling around smoking cigarettes and getting bagels, and nobody batted an eye. You know why? Because it made sense. It was what he was supposed to look like. Dick Stockton, you can do the same thing. It's time. The cat's out of the bag and on your head. Show up to the game for TNT in your jammies and the white cotton slippers you found in the bedding section of Nordstrom's and get your fucking soul in sync. The Brooks Brothers suit doesn't look comfortable, and the "now you see it, now you don't" combover is worrisome. I love you, Dick. Please.

Let me keep it real for a minute. I've struggled with my own hair shit; I know what it is to worry that it's going away. I've felt the beginnings of male pattern baldness. I've run my fingers through my hair and thought, *Where the fuck did it go?* I've taken pills and potions and dyes and dips to keep my shit intact. It's part of the game out here in Hollywood.

You think it's a coincidence that ten out of ten top Hollywood stars have all their hair? Take it from me, kids, there ain't no coincidences at the Hollywood Hair Club for Men. I'm not here to name names, George, Brad, Ben, or Matt, but things just can't be that fucking good. You can't be that talented and rich and naturally have all your hair at forty-five plus. Not all of you fucks. Shit just don't work that way. Especially you, George. I know before bed, you gotta lay that perfect nest on the end table. When was the last time you saw a gigantic trillion-dollar-grossing movie star go bald? Case closed.

But this ain't about movie stars. This is about one-of-a-kind talents with one-of-a-kind voices who should work until the wheels fall off. Marv Albert is seventy-five and he's not replaceable. The man owns the word *Yes*. You can never have another broadcaster say "Yes" when Steph Curry makes a rainbow three-pointer. Only Marv Albert can do that. Get off his head.

Only Hubie Brown and Mike Fratello can riff on the air and go on and on about the brilliance of Pete Maravich and the times when Pistol Pete and Dr. J played one-on-one during ABA practice. They were there. They can't be replaced. They're sports icons.

Why the hell am I the only one bringing up the problem? Why am I the only one it seems to bother so badly? Why am I the only one so damn offended by these wacky wigs and these horrendous horse hairpieces? I shouldn't be alone here. I want you guys to be offended and to get upset here, too. Fuck the wigs and the plugs—you don't need 'em. We are lucky to have you calling games, telling stories, and sharing your lives and points of view. Stand up and get mad! Be fed up and take a stand on live TV. The next time your no-good, hotshot twenty-nine-year-old director in his three-piece clown suit yells "Action," you say, "Fuck you and this wig. I'm done. Now take this ridiculous-looking animal fur off my perfectly shaped yet slightly dented head. I'm not doing this anymore. I'm better than this wig, and I'm better than this oversized suit that never fits!" Look into camera three and tell the world, "I am mad as hell, and I'm not gonna wear this anymore!" I want you to throw the fucking pig wig down and tell your producer to get you a ginger ale and a toasted English muffin and to get the fuck out of your face. Then say it again and say it loud, boys: "I am mad as hell, and I'm not gonna wear this anymore. I am mad as hell, and I'm not gonna wear this anymore!"

For the record, I can't be sure that they all wear toupees, and if I'm wrong, I am sorry . . . about the state of their hair, and I truly love all you guys.

Bill Russell Is Overrated, Deal with It

If you think Bill Russell is "the Best NBA Player Ever," then Skip This Chapter, because I'm here to tell you he ain't. I'm sorry, but your hero Bill Russell is not the best, and he's not the second best, and, no, he's not even the third best. As a matter of fact, he doesn't make the Rapaport Top Ten. Don't get mad at me. It's not my fault your parents and your grandparents have been selling you this shit the same way they sold you on cod liver oil being good for you, when in fact no one knew what the fuck cod liver oil was.

I know you are thinking this is coming from the bitter soul of a disgruntled lifelong New York Knicks fan. But that's not it. Am I a bitter Knicks fan? Without a doubt. Is it difficult to sleep at night knowing that the Knicks were cursed by unknown powers and that they may never be great again in my lifetime? Yes. Does it stick me like a chubby pig before he says good-bye to Earth that the team I love could lose to a high-level college team? Yeah. It hurts. It all hurts. The orange and blue that pumps through my basketball veins is cold, distorted, and angry and ready to have me cancel my NBA package altogether, but hear ye, hear ye, court is in session: Bill Russell is simply fucking overrated.

Listen, I sleep well at night knowing that the first team to beat the Celtics in a game 7 at the original Boston Garden was my 1973 Knicks. I feel good that in the Eastern Conference Finals my childhood heroes went on to win our last NBA title with the most talented team ever assembled. So, don't worry about me. And I'm not denying that Bill Russell dominated his era. I'm just saying you must look at the big picture. You have to look at the kindergarteners he was playing against and rethink whether he was actually great at basketball or whether everyone around him just sucked.

It's true that Bill Russell is the winningest athlete in basketball history. This is something I found out while fact-checking against my will. He was also an eleven-time NBA champion. But it all happened at a time when everyone else was slow and broken. He was shattering records against men who went on to become butchers and orthodontists, who played basketball for side money and all looked like my uncles. Bill's stats don't match the world he was living in. Sorry.

Bill Russell was a five-time NBA MVP. Very impressive. A stat that can't be debated, debunked, or denied. But what can be brought up is the fact that the guy with the next highest vote total was Morrie Fienberg, my dad's foot doctor, who went on to become "the Corned Beef Distribution King of New York," not a Hall of Fame inductee. RIP to Morrie and everyone who died from sodium in the Sixties. Sorry, Bill Russell, it was the era, not the skills.

Bill Russell was also a twelve-time NBA All-Star. That's nothing to scoff at. That's not an easy feat. For twelve years to be one of the best in the NBA is very real and extremely difficult. You have to be at the top of your game every night in every city, and he did that at the highest level. But you know what's more impressive to me? Bruce Jenner won the decathlon, then went home and put on a dress when everyone else was in an ice bath! Why are we not talking about *that* greatness? That's a feat, too.

Bill Russell was named to the first-ever NBA All-Defensive First Team in 1969. The historical Russell was known as a game-changing defensive player, as depicted in this photograph.

Jesus H. Christ, Russ, why don't you pick on somebody your own size? This is nothing to be proud of. The Stevenson Collection/Getty Images

Bill Russell was the NBA rebounding champion in '57, '58, '59, '64, and '65. He was crashing boards and breaking records and doing things no one had seen before him. He could jump higher than everyone he battled in the paint. No one even came close. You know why? Because they weren't full-grown yet. You want to break rebounding records, play against guys before they hit puberty.

Come see me play against my teenage son's friends. I do it every week. It makes me feel good. I get a kick out of it, and it gets my confidence in a perfect place to go on with my difficult week. Every man should play against people he can dominate. It's like the HBO show *Westworld*! I can go in there and do whatever the hell I want. Bill did the same thing. He was playing in a fantasy league.

Number 15 for the Warriors looks like he's five foot ten, 162 pounds, and watching a solar eclipse in sheer awe. Warriors number 17 is running for his life, away from the scene of this unjust crime. The Stevenson Collection/Getty Images

Russell never lost a game 7 or a title game during his career, which means that when the money was on the line in high school, college, the Olympics, or pro, Bill never lost. "Fantastic" and "holy shit," but by game 7, everyone else he was playing against was fucking tired from working their second jobs. You try playing defense against Bill Russell after a full day of selling life insurance door-to-door.

In his rookie season, Russell led the Celtics to the first of eleven NBA titles, an untouchable record that doesn't even sound possible. Something for the ages. A record that to this day shocks fans and statisticians. Also, a record achieved while playing against slow, white, bad-kneed men in a nonintegrated league where each team had only two black players. Come on, Bill, was it that tough?

Mr. Russell led his Celtics to the promised land by conquering the Syracuse Nationals in the Eastern Conference Finals.

The Nats' scorer was Hall of Famer Dolph Schayes. There are no weak Dolphs in the world. That's a fact. Just look at Dolph Lundgren. He fought Rocky and ran around the gym shredded with no fat while on steroids and racism, ready to take on America.

If Dolph Schayes was guarding Bill, then Bill was going to score a lot of points. Dolph was six foot seven, full of gorgeous, thick hair, and he was Jewish. Bill Russell was six foot ten and 220 pounds of solid rock, lean, mean athlete. Dolph was 195 pounds of matzah ball soup. You don't cover Bill Russell well when every Sunday you're knee-deep in bagels and smoked salmon. It's too much.

Of course Russell is gonna pull down 31 rebounds a game against this Giant Jew. Bill moved him out of the way while Dolph thought about going to med school or working in the garment district. Either was fine with him. He knew the deal. It wasn't a fair matchup at all.

Bill Russell led the Celtics in his rookie season to a championship, and the entire thing culminated in a tough game 7 with "the Coleman Play," a play that defined Bill Russell as the "dominating defensive center of his era"—an era rarely caught on tape, which helps with the mythmaking. In fact, many of the NBA's greatest moments weren't preserved on film, TV, or even snapshots. Wilt Chamberlain's 100-point game? I believe it happened, but it has crossed my mind that the whole fucking thing was made up, since no one can seem to find it.

During game 7 of those Finals, and I quote, "Russell ran down Hawks guard Jack Coleman, who received an outlet pass at midcourt, and Russell blocked his shot despite the fact that Russell had been standing at his own baseline when the ball was thrown to Coleman. The block preserved Boston's slim 103–102 lead with forty-odd seconds left to play in regulation, saving the game for the Celtics."

Sounds outstanding, right? Sounds amazing. Sounds like someone made a fucking mistake! How the hell do you get from the baseline to center court on the inbound? Are you a superhero? Are you the fastest man on the planet? Or are you a figment of a sportswriter's imagination? They're making it sound like LeBron's block against Iguodala in game 7 of the 2016 NBA Finals, and it doesn't make any sense in reality! Plus, please take a look at Jack-Fucking-Coleman! Look him up online right now.

Does he look anything like Andre fucking Iguodala? Iguodala was in the 2006 Dunk Contest and has a highlight reel that would make the Late Great Darryl Dawkins blush from the

Planet Love Tron. Jack Coleman looked like he wanted to get home for cheesecake and television. Stop making these guys out to be gods!

Bill Russell wasn't the greatest player of all time. He just happened to be the greatest player of his time.

The iconic Dolph Schayes, in 1959, was a hero in the Jewish community and was once really nice to me when nobody else was. The Stevenson Collection/Getty Images

Dolph Schayes and the Athletic Jews of Yesteryear

If you think I was hating on Jewish athletes in the Bill Russell piece, you could not be more wrong. First off, Dolph Schayes was a Hall of Fame player and one of the many great Jewish athletes from back in the day. There ain't no hate here; I love my people. The Jews made some great accomplishments in sports as athletes. You think I don't know about the Sandy Koufaxes of the world, and the Hank Greenbergs in baseball? You think I don't know there were amazing Jewish boxers in the Thirties, Forties, Fifties, and Sixties who fought for World Championships like Barney Ross and Benny Leonard? I know all about it. We had our day. But it's over. I'm sure one day there will be some Jewish freak of nature who will come along and shock the community and even the world. I know that's a possibility. But please just accept the way things are now. It's over for us in pro sports. I will die in peace having never seen a Jewish tight end starting in the NFL, and that is okay.

Why did it stop? Because as scrappy and determined as my people are, we just ain't built for high-level competitive sports anymore. That's a 100 percent unchecked fact. Once sports became fully integrated, things came to an abrupt end for the Hebes, and it's fine; the "Chosen People" had a good run. But it was just that . . . a run. Now let it go. Look around. When's the last time you heard: "And the gold medal for the two-hundred-yard sprint goes to Aaron Schwartzberg"?

The film *White Men Can't Jump* should've just been called *Jewish Men Are Slow as Fuck, Can't Jump, and Neither Can Gentiles, But They've Got a Few Exceptions*! That's too long for a title, but I'm sure they'd consider it if the movie came out today.

So, I'm not hating on Dolph Schayes. In fact, I know personally that he was a very good man. In 1982, I attended Dolph Schayes's basketball camp in upstate New York. And even though I was threatened with being thrown out four days into camp for disciplinary reasons, Mr. Schayes took me aside and gave me a very fair talking-to. He suggested I play with the older kids to keep me in line, and he ultimately kept me in the camp for the entire seven days despite my counselor's constant attempts to throw me out. They also teased me by calling me RapaCrap the entire session. It was an emotional summer, but Mr. Schayes spoke to me like a loving Jewish Giant Grandfather—something I needed at the time.

"Michael, everything about your behavior this week says you should be thrown out."

"Thank you, coach."

"Michael, this isn't a sentence that requires a thank-you. This is me telling you you should be out of here, and your behavior needs to change."

"Oh, well, then, no thanks?"

"It just means you need to straighten up and fly right. You're not paying any attention at the camp, and you're running into other people's cabins yelling random things like a *meshuggener*."

"I'll stop. I promise. I love basketball."

"No one cares about that. Just take a breath."

"Okay."

"Get it together, Michael. You've got great potential."

"That means a lot. Basketball is everything to me."

"I don't mean in basketball. Basketball is not in your future."

"It's not?"

"No. You're heavy-footed and you don't have the patience to learn the game."

"Well, what am I supposed to do?"

"Let's start with paying attention to the counselors when they talk."

"I don't know."

"I do. Trust me. I see the good in you."

"Thanks."

"Even if I'm the only one who sees it here."

"Shit, man."

No bullshit, Dolph Schayes had my back in '82 when no one else did, and I always appreciated it.

Allen Iverson and the Weeping Woman

Watching my man Allen Iverson play hoops was like watching Jackson Pollock paint. Crazy energy, flailing all over the fucking room, knocking shit over, falling down, half bleeding, sweating, and putting every ounce of his soul on the line every night. And when it was over, you had just witnessed a thing of fucking beauty and you were emotionally exhausted. This is what a real artist does: moves the shit out of you. Of course, there were stronger, faster, bigger, more-skilled players, better shooters, sharper passers, all-around more talented players, and all that other bullshit, but he was the motherfucking king of self-expression! I'm talking about laying it on the line every time he hit the floor and painting the picture that was running through his veins. Leaving everything he had on the court. The same way an artist leaves it on the canvas or a great rapper like 2Pac left it on the track.

I don't get moved by much these days, but when my lady forced me to go to the Museum of Modern Art against my will for a Picasso exhibit called *The Weeping Women*, my first thought while checking out Pablo's work was fucking Iverson is the Picasso of his shit! He was all AI all day! His heart and soul were all over the court, all over every single game he played.

AI wasn't concerned with what you thought. Real artists aren't. John Coltrane didn't ask you what note he was supposed to play when crafting *A Love Supreme*. He played what he felt, and then you came along. AI played his game, lived his way, and you either came along or you didn't. He gave no fucks what you thought, and he still played great.

Iverson played in eleven straight All-Star Games, was the '96 Rookie of the Year, number one in steals two years in a row, and averaged the most points per game in four seasons all while standing six feet tall and weighing 160 pounds fully clothed with three pounds of jewelry and a do-rag.

Yeah, I know he drove his coaches bat-shit crazy and could shoot you in and out of a game in the same half, and I know the "practice rant" seemed off the wall, but he was always, always, always A to the I. And let me be clear: I agreed with him during that rant.

He was on TV during that press conference telling it exactly how it was: "Practice, we in here talking 'bout practice, I'm the franchise player and we talking about practice." This makes total sense to me. He went out every day, busted his ass on the court, put his body and life on the line, and you're asking him about practice? Half the game he's about to crash onto the floor or flying into the stands for an out-of-bounds ball. He needed to take a few days' rest. Plus, AI was your star.

Iverson had the looks, image, and swagger of a superstar. He carried himself like there was a red carpet under him at all times. He was on some real James Dean shit. He should have been the face of the NBA. Who else did they want, Steve Nash? No offense to my man Stevie Nash, but he looks like Kelly Leak, the burnout in the original *Bad News Bears* movie. But I also felt like AI was a genuinely shy person. He didn't want to talk to the press. Why should he want to? He's not a debutante. He's not a gossip. So what, he liked to keep it close to the vest with the press? He just never seemed comfortable, like LeBron and Magic did, when it came to talking to the press, and he made no apologies for it. He was just doing him to the power of 10.

I remember the press was on AI because he said, "Some days I don't feel like going to shoot around. I don't even feel like playing basketball every day." The headlines read that he wasn't grateful to play pro and he didn't care about his team and all sorts of bullshit. He was telling it how it is. The fucking truth. You think anyone likes working at whatever job they have every single day? I don't give a shit if your job is tasting candy, you're not going to love it every day. As much as AI loved playing ball, it's still a JOB. Who the hell loves their job every day? No one. I have a damn cool job, and of course, I love what I do, but are there days when I'd rather be home on the couch with a case of Snapple, drowning myself in processed sugar? Yeah. It happens. It's natural. I don't care if you're in the NBA, NFL, NHL, MLB, CFL, the Rolling Stones, or Coldplay. (I don't know why the hell I threw Coldplay in there. They just seem really happy all the time.) Let a man express the way he feels and move on. AI's honesty bothered you? Too bad. He went hard when he went to work, and that should have been all that mattered.

Iverson wasn't the best shooter, his form was not perfect, and, sure, when he passed, it felt like he was doing it reluctantly, as if saying, "Here, man, but you know I'd rather shoot." He was *one* of the best ball handlers ever, but not the best. His shot selection was off the wall at times, but so the fuck what? He attacked and kept coming relentlessly. All art, all day. He went harder on the floor than anybody every game, every possession, and you felt it!

I don't give a shit; you can teach shooting, passing, and defensive footwork all you want, but you can't teach that inner drive to kick fucking ass every play of every game. You can't teach toughness. There's no class for getting the shit knocked out of your 160-pound body and hopping back up and going at it till you're bleeding. This is something you're born with.

I know Jordan was a savage, and Bird was a cold-blooded killer, and Kobe wanted to step on your throat, but watching Allen Iverson attack was like seeing a live fucking statement. He came out skipping up and down in warm-ups, getting his Me Against the World mentality going in his head, thrashing his body come game time, crashing to the floor, falling out of bounds, smashing into the stands, and then walking away, headband tight, cornrows set, MVP of that game.

Watching Allen Iverson play told you everything you needed to know about him as a person. You could feel his heartbeat. You could feel his pain when he lost and his joy when he was winning.

Watching Iverson play articulated the beauty, pain, chaos, and struggle that made him a true artist on the floor. Thank you, my man. Watching you play made me feel alive every single time, and that's what great art is supposed to do.

The Michael Rapaport Celebrity Scouting Report, Volume 1

By now I'm sure a lot of you are saying to yourselves, "Rapaport, you're talking an awful lot of shit about pro athletes. Does it have anything to do with the fact that you'll never be one?" No, it doesn't, but if it bothers you, then let's take a little break and talk some shit about people I actually know and have played against. So here you have it, the very first "Rapaport Celebrity Scouting Report—Or, Celebs Who Think They Can Ball."

Common

One of the most respected and influential rappers to ever do it, a prolific actor, one of the most well-rounded talents in our industry, and he's never seen a jump shot he didn't like. Gives 100 percent of himself on screen and shoots 100 percent of the time he gets the ball. My man was incredibly believable in *Just Wright* as a pro ballplayer, but something tells me passing wasn't in the script. When he's not shooting a flick or TV piece, he's shooting the rock, whether open or not. I have been open in front of you for six straight years, my friend, and I've never seen a ball near me. I'm open, man—pass me the rock, please. Maybe it was "the incident" that made him this way. If you don't know about "the incident," allow me.

It was the 2011 Celebrity All-Star Game, and our team was playing against Justin Bieber's team. I called a quick pregame huddle and told my squad, Do not allow Bieber to cross you over or make you look bad, because the public will know about it, and, worse yet, your friends will never let you live it down. I even said foul the Canadian Jack Rabbit if you have to, but do not let him make you look bad. Well, when we came out of the time-out, Common reached out to D up the frail pop icon and got crossed over, ankles broken, and straight shook by the singer. Common took it on the chin but went on to do enough quality work that "the incident" is rarely, if ever, brought up. Sorry for bringing it up, my man.

Justin Bieber

Small, scrappy, unpredictable, and Canadian. He makes great use of his dancing feet as well. I played against Bieber in the 2011 Celebrity All-Star Game, where I was trying to go back to back as the MVP. It wasn't meant to be that year due to a toe issue I never brought up. Bieber was quicker and more competitive than expected but made countless unnecessary extra moves, showing off for the screaming girls who showed up. He dribbled between his legs while no one was checking him and went behind the back twice alone. I have to admit he took a few hard fouls from me and handled them like a champ. He popped right up off the floor like a backup dancer who fell during a Grammy performance and wasn't going to be embarrassed. Biebs took MVP that year. Good shit, bro.

Ice Cube

A Top Five or Top Ten MC on anybody who knows anything about rap music's best-of list. Rapper turned mogul. Brains of the operation. My costar in *Higher Learning*, and even threw me a dope cameo bone in *Next Friday*. However, he also rapped, "Get me on the court and I'm trouble, last week fucked around and got a triple double" in a song. Great lyric, kinda, sort of hard to believe. Cube can legit play; don't get it twisted. However, I've balled with Cube, and I need to see some tape of this triple double. Not saying it didn't happen; I'm just saying I wouldn't mind an eyewitness or even some verbal proof that this alleged triple double didn't just rhyme with the word *trouble*. Ice Cube really does have a tricky old-school game. He's not shy about calling for the ball or shooting the rock, and he will absolutely run down-court before seeing if it goes in the hoop. His confidence sort of outweighs his ability, but if everything I touched turned to gold, platinum, and box-office bonanzas, I'd be crazy confident, too.

Tobey Maguire

Solid actor, but his competitive nature doesn't match his skill set. Goes hard every single play, just not sure where he's going. Nearly kills himself and everyone in his path with or without the ball. Tobey plays hoops like he's running from a fire and isn't sure who to tell about it—frantic, rolling around on the ground for loose balls, and periodically diving for a ball that's not there. Hypercompetitiveness works to his advantage. If you like scrappy reckless abandon, you want him on your squad.

Adam Sandler

Sandler is passively aggressive and oddly deceiving. He's got the same game as the old guy on the court with the black socks high above the calf business and gym-teacher nut huggers from the Seventies. Sandler looks like everyone's uncle, then buries you for twenty without sweating. Great low Jewish center of gravity mixed with slow feet that somehow find the perfect position to score. His thousands of hours of "lunch breaks on set" basketball paid off. He's got true-blue "box out" ass and an uncanny knack for making passes that look fucked up when they leave his hands but somehow find their man.

Brian McKnight

Grammy-winning singer who can croon a girl's panties off, trick her into liking you, and then dunk on her brother. McK-nice can shoot the lights out from three-point land, and the release looks as smooth as he sounds. Also impressive is his ability to take it to the hole and go hard. He drove by me once and whispered some R&B shit like Isaac Hayes. He crossed me over, and all I heard was, "I didn't want to have to do this to you, but I did, Michael." However, he is a ball hog. That solo artist life's got you forgetting about good old-fashioned team ball.

Drake

Rap skills are solid, the voice is original, the dedication to the craft is strong, but he shot a fucking airball during warm-ups for the Kentucky Wildcat game, and I can't let that slide. Drake's game is fast and slow at the same time. His hands move fast while his feet go slow. It's tough to explain, but it may be some Canadian post–Bar Mitzvah shit.

Kanye

Yeezus rented the entire Staples Center for his birthday, and the shit backfired. All reports have Bieber winning MVP once again that day, and my sources tell me Kanye wasn't happy about it and tossed out Bieber's gift to him at the party. Kanye's game is all shoulders and sprinting for no reason. His inability to find the open man has more to do with him not looking than it does with his passing skills. No reports, videos, or cell phone footage can be found of the day Bieber stole Yeezy's b-day from him.

Will Ferrell

Amazing center of gravity, strange amount of athleticism from a body that doesn't scream sports, and the low-post game is bafflingly solid. Hands down the funniest athlete in the world, he is nearly impossible to defend due to laughter. Every play is another *SNL* skit. He uses humor on offense and defense, which gives him a hilariously well-rounded game.

Leo

Number one on my All-Time Great Stickmen list, so it irks me that he's also got a solid post-up game developed while training for *The Basketball Diaries*. His expensive trainer taught him a pivot spin move that he still uses fifteen years later and is tough to defend. Leo's got long arms, and when it looks like he's nowhere near you, somehow he's hand checking you. Thank God his jumper is absolutely nonexistent; otherwise he'd be too perfect a human.

Mark Wahlberg

Excellent actor, real-deal media mogul, could run for office at this point but should take some time off running on the hoop court. Mark's got speed, agility, and strength, but they all belong in football, rugby, or street fighting. The finesse game is not his thing, and he's been known around town to call suspect fouls that are still talked about in celebrity circles. I played with him during the Marky Mark and the Funky Bunch days, and there wasn't one thing funky about his basketball skill set. However, Wahlberg's work ethic is undeniable, so I would never count him out.

Kevin Hart

Once had fantastic speed and incredible athleticism. Now both are gone and have been replaced with humor and wealth. The Philly native had a legit all-around aggressive game equipped with handles and lockdown defense. K Hart is impressive at five foot six, with no fear of driving the lane with the big boys of normal height. I hate to say it, but Father Time has stolen both the quickness and the vertical. It may be that you're weighed down by the massive box office receipts or the millions in cash, but the facts are the facts, and the days of lightning quickness and fearless drives are behind you. Congrats on being the new king of comedy, but now we're the same speed, so I'll see you when I see you.

Queen Latifah

The Queen's game is no joke. Not afraid to mix it up with mere mortals and bang in the paint. La goes hard with either hand and will have you scratching your head and confused by the fadeaway. It's original. It looks like she's falling down backward, but she's actually fading away. If she shows up in the ponytail, you're through. Not one for trash talking, I've seen her bust 23 and leave without talking to anyone before, during, or after the game.

Woody Harrelson

White Men Can't Jump in real life either. Played with him a bunch. He's scrappy, and his jumper is disjointed yet somehow on point. He looks like he's tripping over a curb when he shoots. It's impossible to block his shot because even he doesn't know where it's coming from. Loves to talk shit and won't back down. Strangely strong calves, but his finger roll at the net isn't as good as his joint-rolling skills on the bus.

Wood Harris

The Wire's Avon Barksdale is legit on the court and has a shit-talking game that's easily on par with his acting game. His oversized Doctor J hands that seem too big for his body are his greatest assets. I've seen him dunk on fellow SAG and DGA members with odd slow-motion yet impressive one-handed slams that left the union members stunned and upset about their own game.

Nick Cannon

Multitalented TV mogul and an underrated stickman, Nick can play almost as well as he dresses. He comes fresh as can be, hair tight, shoes on point, and two shirts minimum per game. Solid fadeaway but lazy on D. On D, he looks like he's thinking about hosting another show. Nick's got too many jobs to be great at hoops these days.

George Clooney

I once lost a best of three one-on-one series to George on his personal Warner Bros. court during his days on *ER*, but I was off that day and played without breakfast. Questionable calls were made, but he won fair and square, pretty much. George's game is confusing because he'll foul you, talk smack, and then be friendly. It's a real mind fuck. Also in my defense, George was making a million an episode at the time, and the fear of injuring him hampered my usual aggressive style that would have locked him down. Plus, I didn't want to scar the face of the Sexiest Man Alive. Something about him being so handsome and sweating on me took my mind out of the game. The fucker beat me two out of three and went on talk shows and bragged about it. My street cred hasn't been the same since.

Breckin Meyer

Short, fiery game, and does an uncomfortable amount of running around. The guy never stops moving, even in a half-court game. He's running around somewhere right now for the hell of it. I guarantee it.

Sacha Baron Cohen

Borat is one funny dude, but unfortunately hoops is not his thing. Post-up game is confusing because he's tall in position yet looks completely lost. His jumper is nowhere, but he's such a nice guy that I feel bad athletics didn't make it into his genes.

Dean Cain

Superman can ball. Heavy-handed and big-bodied when he's thinned out, Cain's got a legit jumper and can run the point if he has to. Great court vision, and his hair is fucking amazing.

Denzel

Balled against him years ago at the YMCA, and he always brought his outdoor game indoors. Behind-the-back passes and long-range jumpers followed by quick shit talking; he was well rounded out there. He's also oddly strong, and I can see why he breaks shit in every movie. He plays like he's always on the verge of pushing you down.

Jaleel White

Urkel could ball for real. Solid handles, good fadeaway, tight jumper, never hogged the rock, but the fact that he was Urkel fucked a lot of people's heads up on the parquet floor, especially when he was talking smack.

Will Smith

Great dude, solid game, yet lacked a little speed. Respectable Philadelphia-style game. Hates playing defense, but a deceptively strong lower body. His wind was suspect until he did the movie *Ali*. After *Ali*, the Fresh Prince was too rich to play in public, and there are no up-to-date scouting reports.

#MadShaming

MAD SHAMING: (*verb*) When a person tries to cover up feelings of being pissed the fuck off to avoid the shame of showing anger in public.

One of the best and most scandalous examples of public Mad Shaming was when the Seattle Seahawks beat the Patriots in 2013, and the first-ballot, shit-talking Hall of Famer Richard Sherman ran over to Tom Brady and asked this question: "You mad, bro, you mad?" and Tom Brady didn't respond. Not a word. But you could see on his face that Tom was thinking, Yeah, you fuck, of course I'm mad. We just lost, I played like shit, and your dumb ass intercepted me, and now you're running over to me with some passive-aggressive bullshit asking me if I'm mad? Yeah, I'm fucking mad, bro, I'm really fucking mad. Now take a walk, fucknuts, before I smack one of those dreads off your head, bro.

Now, it's very well documented that I can't stand Tom Fucking Brady, but in that moment, I was on his side 100 percent. Because that "You mad, bro, you mad" from Richard Sherman was straight up MAD SHAMING. It was captured on camera and laid out in very basic terms. Tom Brady did not and would not articulate his true feelings of anger and frustration because of his fear of showing feelings in public, and he was very publicly and very mercilessly Mad Shamed.

The Richard Sherman Mad Shaming incident was replayed over and over and over for weeks on sports shows. It became its own hashtag, #YouMadBro, and somebody even opened an @YouMadBro account on Twitter. Am I Mad, Bro? You bet your sweet fucking ass I'm mad, prick lips, but the fuck if I'm going to show it right now. Why? I ask. Why not show it? Why not get mad? Go ahead, get mad, get real mad, and embrace it, people.

This Mad Shaming needs to stop now. Anger is great, it's natural. I feel it right now for no reason at all. Being mad is fantastic, and being Mad Shamed is not okay—plus it has deep ramifications on its victims in ways only well-trained doctors can diagnose. It's embarrassing, regrettable, terrible for your health, and, above all, downright shameful.

Embrace your anger, embrace your madness. Stand up against Mad Shaming and let the tiger roar, let the lion out, and if the bear is poked, go ahead and say, "Fuck it," and let the bear take a swipe. Stop holding it all in. That's what causes bad behavior in the outside world, not to mention chronic diarrhea.

Mad Shaming is beyond sports. It's happening every day in schools, in the workplace, and in the home. We're all so afraid to show our anger out of fear of people pointing and taunting and saying passive-aggressive shit like "Wow, are you getting upset, dude?" Guess what? Yeah, motherfucker, I'm getting upset. I'm even more upset at the fact that I can't show how upset I am, and it's about to manifest itself later in my day, and I'm going to take it out on someone who doesn't deserve it, so yeah, I Am Upset, Dude.

I'm getting more upset that you're even asking me if I'm getting upset, with that Rob Lowe peaceful-looking resting smirk on your face. No disrespect to Rob Lowe, but he knows that his smirk could drive a motherfucker crazy if it just stared at you asking if you were upset. But shout-out to Rob Lowe's skin lotion. My man looks good for being three thousand years old.

The entire *Incredible Hulk* series was based on Mad Shaming. The poor prick David Banner couldn't feel anger, and if he did, he turned into a giant green beast who whooped the fuck out of everyone in sight. If he could have just felt his anger and expressed it, he wouldn't have had to turn green, turn into Lou Ferrigno, and have us act like it was the same guy.

Now don't forget that Mad Shaming is the cousin of Hate Shaming. Every day you hear people question variations of Hating: Why you hating? You're a hater. Don't hate. I strongly believe that you can't truly love if you can't truly hate. Hating in sports is healthy. Hating in sports is essential. Being a fan of competitive sports is one of the only places that I think some good old-fashioned healthy hate should be embraced and encouraged. Now, you wanna humiliate people because of their organic, god-given hate? You want to take this away from people? You wanna dishonor and disgrace people because of this? No! Stop it now. Stop it right fucking now.

It's an enormous part of sports. Maybe one of my favorites. Saying "Don't hate" in sports is like saying "Don't love." You can't love if you don't hate. It's simple mathematics. Ask the Dalai Lama. He started out as a hater. Or one of those guys did before they started walking around in nice robes loving everyone and half smiling. The Shaolin monks were violent haters until they went the way of the peaceful warrior. Look it up. I don't know if any of this is totally correct, but I'm in the flow, and I don't fact check.

I wouldn't dare attempt to stop a Red Sox fan from hating

Bucky Dent. You should hate him. Never would I talk shit to a pissed-off, swollen-faced Boston Red Sox fan and say some punk-ass Hate Shaming shit like "Why are you hating on Bucky Dent?" Don't be mad that New York Yankee Bucky Dent hit that looping home run over that dingy-ass Green Monster in that hellhole you call Fenway Park.

I know exactly why all Boston fans hate the Buckster. I would never take that away from even the most venomous, low-life Boston Red Sox fan while he's sauced up and crying about his team. I get it. It's the same reason why I hate that cockeyed bastard David Ortiz. Who can hate the lovable Big Papi? Me, that's who. Oh, and every single Yankees fan alive. It's okay. Sports lovers love to hate. It's in our blood. Of course, we respect that fat motherfucker, but we also hate that motherfucker. We have to. And it makes perfect sense. Respecting and hating have nothing and everything to do with each other. I don't hate any lames. I only hate the greats.

You think I spent time loving Michael Fucking Jordan during his career? Hell, no. Of course I knew he was the best player ever, and I stayed up late to watch his highlights on every news channel early in his career. Of course I loved and wore his sneakers, like the rest of the world. But that was all before he became a real fucking issue for me. Once he started kicking the New York Knicks' asses, it was over. All of it. There went the Jordan posters on my wall, right into the fucking garbage. No more running around New York to buy overpriced Jordans, and no more humming the "Be Like Mike" song. I didn't wanna be like Mike—I wanted to bury Mike. I hated that fuck. I despised him. I was blinded by hate, disgust, and anger. I didn't cheer for MJ when he came back to the Garden in '95 and dropped 55 on us. I was pissed off, and I know for damn sure that Jordan loved the hate. It made him great. The greats embrace the hate.

Reggie Miller lived off visceral, raging hate from fans in every arena in every city. He would drink hate smoothies for breakfast. He ate, drank, and shat hate sandwiches. Without that hate, Reggie Miller doesn't make the Hall of Fame. Reggie "the Fuck" Miller would never question fans being angry toward him; it was his fuel and his fire. I couldn't stand that snaggletoothed cocksucker. A few years after Reggie retired, I saw him in a restaurant in New York City and walked over to him. Before I could say anything, he said, "You ready to give it up, you ready to stop hating and stop talking shit?" It wasn't at all mean or confrontational. He had seen me at games over the years heckling and knew I had hated his fucking guts throughout his career. Now he was asking me if I was ready to put down my sword and treat him with normal person-to-person respect. I told him straight up, "Reggie, I hated you to death, but I respected you even more." We gave each other a pound, and that was it. When I see him now around at NBA games, it's all love, but we both know that old hate never fades.

Joe Montana killed the Giants game after game, and I hated him and his fucking amazing hair and dimples. That Goofy-Ass, Stretch Armstrong–looking Randy Johnson taking away the Yankees' World Series in 2001? The hate and disgust I felt toward him was real and vital, and if I saw him today, it would be tough to not say something. The guy stole months of my happiness, and it stung. But guess what? It's okay. It's what makes sports so damn entertaining and such an amazing escape. We get to feel it all, and it's okay. So, next time you or somebody else is screaming and yelling with snot coming out of their nose because their favorite player or team took a tough loss, sit back and let them go through the natural progressions of being mad as fuck and let them hate as hard as they need to until it passes naturally. It's just nature taking its course. Embrace the hate.

Question Time for Bill Belichick

Bill Belicheat, what can I say? Billy Boy, I don't like you. I don't like your face. I find it quite unsettling. I don't like your disposition or the way you've carried yourself all these years, Bill. I know you're the winningest NFL coach of all time, but I think you're 500 percent full of caca. Yes, yes, I know that sounds harsh, and I'm sure most of you reading this know I'm not a New England Patriots fan. The easy way out is to assume that my dislike of Billy Bullshit is due to jealousy of the fantastic football team he coaches. That is an incorrect assumption regardless of the fact that I'm a homegrown New York Giants fan. Although we haven't had the undisputable success of the Patriots, I still rejoice, usually during a solid and healthy bowel movement, over the fact that the Giants did two fantastic Super Bowl stuff jobs on New England. They stuffed them nice and they stuffed them proper on the biggest stage in all of sports. Let's take a quick trip down memory lane in case you forgot.

The year was 2008 and the game was Super Bowl XLII, which means Super Bowl 42. To be honest, I had to look up what the fuck XLII equals in the real world of numbers. I don't know why the NFL continues this roman-numeral charade, but this ain't

Game of Thrones, so cut the crap: everyone is lost and googling the roman numerals.

Let's refocus. 2008: the Patriots were being considered the greatest football team ever, and they were close to completing a perfect 19–0 season. Wouldn't that have been delightful? They would be the first team to pull it off since the 1972 Dolphins. Wouldn't that have been a grand accomplishment? Yeah, well, it didn't happen, fuckos. The Giants came into this Super Bowl a huge underdog. They fought their way into the Big Dance and they made it, tattered and torn. New England was up 14–10 at the half. However, New York stayed alive and got the ball back with almost two minutes to go when the Giants' quarterback, the funny-faced, goofy-looking yet stellar Eli Manning, escaped the menacing grip of six or seven Patriot defenders. Baby-faced Eli got loose and threw a duck to David Tyree. The relatively unknown Tyree made a magical catch, pinning the ball to his helmet. He looked as shocked as the rest of the world. I, for one, jumped up on my couch, took my shirt off, scared the shit out of both my sons, and said, "What the fuck! What the fuck!" I doubt any Patriots fans jumped onto their couches during that magical moment, but I'd bet they flipped them over. On the very next play, the Giants quarterback with the inability to grow facial hair threw an easy touchdown to a wide-open Giant receiver named Plaxico Burress. To this day, I still can't figure out why Plaxico was so wide open. I think it was because the Patriots were still in shock from the David Tyree once-in-a-lifetime earmuff catch. Eli Manning was named MVP of the game. Most gamblers would've expected the staggeringly handsome man of steel, the hair-gelled Tom Brady, to be the MVP, but he wasn't. Sorry, Tommy. The Giants won the Super Bowl 17–14, and the Patriots' dreams of being considered the greatest team ever went right down the fucking drain.

And just in case you forgot, the Giants also beat the Patriots in Super Bowl XLVI, which I think means 46, but who the hell knows? I left my roman numeral translator at home again. New York got to the 2012 Super Bowl with the worst record a team ever had at 9–7. Madonna was the halftime guest of honor and flip-flopped around the stage half naked while hanging on for dear life in four-inch heels. I remember staring at the TV praying she didn't tear a meniscus or tweak a hammy.

It wasn't a very memorable game. However, Eli did get a chance to play the hero again, and he did. He threw a pin-perfect pass to Mario Manningham that left the Patriots and their fans in shock and awe. The Giants soon scored what would turn out to be the game-winning touchdown. The Giants' Super Bowl victory was embarrassingly overshadowed by Leonardo DiCaprio's ex-girlfriend and Tom Brady's current wife, Gisele, throwing a postgame shit fit in broken English about Brady's wide receivers dropping catches. It was some lowbrow TMZ shit, but a great moment for all Giant fans. So, like I said, I'm good with where the G-Men stand versus the Patriots. It's Billy Belichick and his attitude I need to talk about.

Billy, Billy, Billy, I know I'm not alone. I have a few questions, and I want some answers. What has crawled up that dusty ass of yours and died, Bill? Why the one-word answers all the time? The robotic Rain Man "I'm just here to coach football" act is tired. It's also rude. You make San Antonio Spurs coach Gregg Popovich look like the life of the party. You know how hard that is to do? For the last seventeen years, every time you show up at a press conference, you've been bad-mannered and impolite to every reporter. You treat every question like it's the dumbest thing you've ever heard. Don't you know that the only dumb question is the one you don't ask, Bill? You're Question Shaming these innocent reporters day after day, week after week, season after season. You're making reporters feel bad about themselves. We get it. You're not a people person, you're a pro football coach, you're just there to do your job, yeah, yeah, yeah. Those reporters you give reluctantly mumbled one-word answers to are just doing their jobs, too. I've been trying to get an NFL-approved press pass so I can show up at your press conferences and ask some questions myself. Thus far, for some reason, my requests have been denied. However, if I ever do get the press lanyard, here are the questions you can expect:

The great Vince Lombardi, legendary leader of men, would show up to games looking sharp and presentable, wearing a pressed suit and tie and that classy wool hat that yelled "dapper leader." Why do you have to show up looking like you just escaped a methadone clinic? Do you understand that people pay hard-earned money to see your successful team play football, yet you're on the sidelines dressed in that dingy cut-off sweatshirt that appears to have been ripped from a puppy's mouth? What the fuck, Bill? Do you own a suit or not?

My second question—do you have any suggestions for a good video camera and lens package? I plan on recording the practice of my son's archrival flag football team. They're a competitive team named the Jets. Would you suggest a camera that assures me the best quality recording to study the Jets in hopes of beating them, despite the fact that I know recording another team's practice is both ethically and morally wrong? Something with a tight rack focus to see all the play-calling signals to assure my son's team a victory would be great. Not saying you would ever do this, but hypothetically, if you were filming another team's practice, what kind of camera would you use?

Finally, have you gotten any handwritten letters from President Trump lately? If so, would you please tell us what the letters were about?

I feel like these are all very reasonable and well-thought-out questions. I'm sure I wouldn't get any answers, because Billy the Grump Hole acts like he doesn't have to answer to anybody. Not sure if you know about this, but there was a very famous mobster from New York City named Vinny "the Chin" Gigante who ran the infamous Genovese Family. His claim to fame was that he walked around Greenwich Village and Little Italy dressed in a bathrobe, pajamas, and slippers and talked to himself when he knew people were watching. He did this to give the impression that he was mentally ill and harmless and not a threat instead of the dangerous, devious criminal he was. Billy "the Chin" Belichick, I'm watching you, I'm not alone, and I'm waiting for my answers.

Hookers, Pills, Dwarfs, and the Las Vegas Raiders

The Oakland Fucking Raiders mean a lot to professional football. They represent something to the game. They have fans who go to literal war for their team. They've bred real football characters and villains in their time. Al Davis ran a passion-filled squad out of Oakland where players like Howie Long, Marcus Allen, Kenny "the Snake" Stabler, and real-life goons like John Matuszak and Jack Tatum thrived under the Raider banner. Matuszak was in the World's Strongest Man contest just for shits and giggles, and Jack Tatum's nickname was the Assassin. Bo Jackson was running over grown men like they were babies, and Lyle Alzado was ripping helmets off other players' heads and throwing them into the stands twelve years after his Bar Mitzvah while hopped up on juice! This was the Raiders of Oakland, California. This was the most hated franchise in all of sports, and for all the right fucking reasons. And now we're about to see this team be hated for all the wrong reasons. Have you ever fucking been to Vegas? Whatever Happens in Vegas Happens for Real in Vegas, and it includes hookers, pills, midgets, and handcuffs. Al "Just Win, Baby" Davis is up there in Black and Silver Heaven freakin' the fuck out. He knows what the hell happens in Vegas. You want to put a bunch of NFL players with money in their pockets and time on their hands in Sin City? Well, let me paint you a not-nice picture of what goes on down here, my friends. I hate to be the bearer of bad fucking news, but let's get real.

First off, their coach, Jack Del Rio, is a passionate guy, and when passion meets a twenty-four-hour playground where pills and pussy are chasing you deep into the night like a devil on steroids, shit can go south quickly. And he's just the coach. Coach comes home, team took a tough loss, the bright lights of the strip start calling his name, and next thing he knows, he's knee-deep in vodka at the craps table and threatening a guy who's making fun of the team. He didn't see it coming. He's not a superhero, he's just a football coach, which already means he's got a screw loose for shit that's loud, dangerous, and wild. That's all the Raiders need is to wonder why Coach Del Rio is living in that cheap motel off the strip and three of his cheerleaders are on the back of a milk carton because they were sold into a Colombian sex-trafficking ring after a loss to the Browns. This is the kind of shit that happens all the time in Vegas. Are you kidding me? I left dealing with credit card fraud and whooping cough. Vegas is the fucking devil's playground!

Las Vegas is also going to be terrible for NFL players. They have a hard enough time staying out of trouble as it is. Take a young player like Tyrell Adams, who's never seen a building taller than his high school, and now he's got the finest girl he's ever seen that wants to "show him around" Vegas and introduce him to her friends at the club. Can you say, "Give me your wallet, I'm having your baby"? What happens when quarterback Derek Carr, a seemingly nice kid who played at Fresno State, a town where people cry over sheep getting shaved, has a bad night and the meth bandits come creeping out of the Luxor? "Psst, Derek, come here, man, try this, it won't kill ya." Fuck that. Amari Cooper, nice kid fresh off the country boat from Alabama, misses two catches and heads through the casino with his head hanging low, and who is there to pick up his spirits? Donna, who last Tuesday was Joe. And now he's got a tranny mistake on his record, and his entire family is calling to make sure he's okay. It's not a good place for these kids, man, I'm telling you. They're targets. And don't tell me how Vegas is family friendly now. These people put the kids to bed and step into a puddle of cocaine and blackjack until they turn into vampires.

Fuck this move, man. Mark Davis, what are you thinking? I know in your mind you think you're going to school the kids and make sure they know who to trust and who not to talk to and all that, but they're men.

I don't care how many guest speakers they bring in to the team to warn kids off the downfall of drugs and hookers in Vegas. The shit is at their fingertips. At least in Oakland you had to cross a bridge, and it wasn't in your face. You had to find a Starbucks with a strong Wi-Fi connection to meet a lady of the night. In Vegas, they're your fans, and next thing you know, they're your employees. This is a shitstorm waiting to happen.

The Oakland Raiders had real grit, real personality, and real fucking edge. What the hell is Vegas's personality? What the hell is the brand now? Who the hell are the VIP guests at home games? The cast of *The Beatles Love* show? Louie Anderson and David Copperfield? Sinatra, Sammy Davis, and Elvis have left the building, my friends. What the hell is it gonna look like when the camera pans up to Mark Davis's suite and it's full of clowns, monkeys, ballerinas, and mimes? Oh, and look who's in the suite today: it's Monte the Tiger and Bobo the Fuckin' Clown from *The O Show*. It does not fit the Raider brand! Oh shit, is that Chris Angel in a half shirt and makeup with a woman cut in half up there? How cute. People want fucking Raider Nation, man!

And what about the cheerleaders? You think your cheerleaders are going to be happy making $150 a game in that town? Sorry for the newsflash, but if you're good-looking, great at dancing, can do the splits, and you're a female in Vegas, there's a little job called stripping that can make you a millionaire in twenty-six months. Who the fuck is going to pick prancing around on Sundays for twelve dollars an hour when you can go to Crazy Horse 4 on a Wednesday afternoon for brunch and walk out with four grand and an offer to fly on a private jet to Cancun? Hmm, should I spend the week coordinating a dance to a Bruno Mars song for a third-quarter routine or walk to Olympic Garden, do some splits, and listen to some fat fuck millionaire while he eats chicken tenders and offers to pay my mortgage? I know what I would do. Yeah me, Michael Rapaport. I'd go there right now in a pink dress and dance my ass off for three grand an hour. Fuck it, life is short. I'll feed him the chicken tenders myself.

What kind of fans will the Raiders have in Vegas? Whoever the fuck puts money down on them to win. If the Raiders don't cover the spread, they won't have fans. They miss a field goal, they lose a fan. At least the Oakland Raiders had loyal-to-the-bone, true-blue gangster fan shit going on over there. They lived by a code, on some real G shit. N.W.A rocked Raider gear as a tribute to Raider Nation and what it represented. Trust me when I tell you you're gonna be begging for the Mexican gangs to be your fans again. You don't want a gang full of degenerate gamblers and derelicts as your fan base. Yeah, I get it, there are real people and families in Vegas blah blah fucking blah. Let's be honest. I'd rather have five hundred members of random street gangs having my back than a crew of cab drivers and toothless roulette players. I don't know, man. The shit just makes no sense to me, and the shit makes no sense to some of the best fans in pro sports.

The Las Vegas Raiders? Get the fuck outta here with that bullshit.

Shame on you!!!!

Fa Fa Fantasy Football

Up until 2014 I thought fantasy football was a fucking joke. I thought it was some stat nerd, *Dungeons & Dragons*, goofball, computer-geek foolishness for backdoor creeps who never played sports and definitely never played real-life tackle football. I thought it was for chumps to take out their frustrations after years of being headhunted in schoolyard dodge ball. Nonetheless, I never played it, never wanted to play it, and considered it really stupid.

All of that changed when a man named Gary Dell'Abate, executive producer of *The Howard Stern Show*, invited me to join the Stern Show Fantasy Football League. If you don't know Mr. Dell'Abate by his government name, you may know him as Baba Booey or the Horse-Toothed Jackass or maybe Fla Fla Flunky. These are all nicknames Gary has been given over the years by the Stern show staff and fans. Nonetheless, being a big fan of *The Howard Stern Show* and knowing that my twelve-year-old son, Maceo, and his best friend, Gray, actually did play fantasy football, I thought it would be harmless fun. So, since fantasy football isn't actual football, it's just a fantasy, and since the Stern show league was only $150 per person buy in with no big prizes at stake, I assumed the camaraderie between the fantasy players win, lose, or draw would be worth the experience. I could let the twelve-year-olds do the drafting and handle my team and all the football operations, and I, of course, could sit back, have a good time, and focus on the real-world shit.

I joined the Stern league with no intentions or thoughts of winning, but once the season started, something changed. Something awoke from the depths of my innards, something I didn't know existed in me. A raging, erupting, competitive, shit-talking, knuckle-dragging fantasy football gorilla emerged. I was addicted, and it wasn't even about the game. I didn't understand the scoring, I didn't understand how my team could win or lose—the shit felt too mathematical. And I hate math. However, my friends, what I did understand was that I had a primal need to talk shit, antagonize, and mind fuck everyone in my fantasy football path. The craziest and realest thing was that I didn't care about winning at all. I just wanted that ass-crackin' action.

Gorilla Mouth Gary Dell'Abate was my main target, because that's just the nature of the man. He has a quality that has brought out harassment and verbal assaults from people, friends, and complete strangers for over thirty years. That's not an opinion, it's a fact. There's just something about Fa Fa Fooey's disposition that makes you wanna fuck with him, and I did. Oh yes, I did, and I did it with the purest form of joy. I started sending group emails to the league, telling Gary that I was gonna beat his team's ass, and even if I lost, I was gonna have my way with him emotionally and insinuated potential sexual experiences we would share . . . as men . . . together . . . intimately.

I know that sounds lewd, crass, and potentially threatening, but there's something very traditional about telling another man you're gonna sexually violate him when it comes to friendly shit talking. And, as Fantasy God is my witness, none of this was premeditated; it just flowed organically from my core and felt as natural as breathing air. The more Gary—or Fa Fa, as I prefer to call him—would respond to me, the more excited I would get and the more graphic my emails would become. The one that seemed to confuse him the most was when I told him I was lurking outside his window with duct tape, a Wonder Bread bag, and some olive oil, and I needed some alone time with him. Although none of this was real, Fa Fa took it seriously, and I was in heaven.

I was having a ball with fantasy football, and my team, which I named Rapaport's DeLight, a.k.a. A History of Violence, a.k.a. Make It Stop Make It Stop, a.k.a. That Thing's Big, started winning. I didn't have anything to do with my team's success; the entire decision making was being done by my twelve-year-old and his friend. Obviously I had to step in and take all the credit, because what else does a great shit talker do to back up the mouth? Real Shit Talkers Do Real Things, and I did. I took full credit from two twelve-year-olds. Fuck it. They have their whole futures in front of them. I was having the time of my life.

A few weeks into the season, this whole thing was being played out on the Howard Stern radio show. I would call in and talk shit to Gary and the rest of the people in the league whose names I'll never mention. Why should I give them shout-outs in my first-ever, soon-to-be-bestselling, already-considered-a-classic sports book? I'm gonna let them live in unknown hidden infamy for now. Anyway, those unmentionable faceless, nameless, hopeless fucks would get on the radio and complain about the content of my numerous emails and try to discredit Rapaport's DeLight's success and say the kids were doing all the work. They said I was just sneaking in and taking all the credit, which was 100 percent true, but I was in my element now. I was like a happy little homeless pig who finally found a warm bed of shit to roll around in.

Talking shit and breaking balls is my comfort zone, and has been my entire life. Hanging out in the streets of New York City talking shit—or snapping, which is what most people I hung with called it—was an everyday thing, and it was something I looked forward to. And if you were good at snapping on people, it was like having a superpower, like having a special skill set like playing basketball or fist fighting or rhyming. Snapping on people would essentially keep the others at arm's length, and I always had a knack for it. I got off on the competitiveness, and some people's feelings got hurt. That's too bad, because the one thing you need to know when it comes to high-level shit talking is that you can never take anything personally. But some do, my friend. Some just do. It's in their DNA.

Enter Matthew Berry

ESPN's Matthew Berry is the world's most famous fantasy football expert and a good guy. He's also a true-blue fantasy football snob, and I don't blame him at all. He's making a great living off the fantasy of football. He's a well-known sports personality who most of the fantasy football world turns to for advice about a game based on a real sport that he may never have played, in any form. It's a beautiful thing, what he's able to do, but I immediately felt like he didn't take me seriously as an opponent. Why should he? I had no idea what I was doing, and I had two twelve-year-olds draft my entire team and handle the work. What can I say? They were the brains of the operation, and I was the brawn. But underestimating Rapaport's DeLight pushed me into fantasy football shit-talking greatness the likes of which no one in the league had ever seen. I chopped Berry down to size immediately because I had to. As soon as I found out he requires you to call him Matthew and not Matt, how do you think I reacted? I think you know. His name immediately became Matt to me. Matt, I'm Gonna Fucking Berry You! Dick move to some. The game within the game to me. That, along with berating him on social media, emails, and the Stern show, worked miracles on Fantasy Matt. One of my favorite fantasy football shit-talking moments came when Berry and I both called in to the Stern show and got into it. We were all arguing and talking shit, but Matt kept at it. He was saying things like "Your team did well, but you don't know anything about football. Your kid and his friend did all the work and yada fucking yada." I don't speak Yada.

I told him with great articulation and in no uncertain terms, "We beat you this season, we fucked you nice, and we fucked you twice. We ripped your heart out, and fuck you." Berry came back with a subtle "Who cares? You didn't do anything to help win the games, and you're taking all the credit." Not true, Matt. It's not easy to count the value of shit-talking in the league, my friend. My final response to him was "You can call it whatever you want, you fantasy fucking nerd, but you either lost to me, a guy who openly admits to knowing absolutely nothing about this game you're an expert at, or you lost to two twelve-year-olds who at the same time they were whooping that ass were studying for their finals. However you want to slice it up, we dethroned you." There was silence for a beat, and the silence was euphoric. That was a win to me. That was a high-level championship ball-breaking win.

Losing in Fantasy Hurts in Real Life

Shockingly, my team made it to the Super Bowl of the Emotional Friends of Stern Show League in my first season there, but we came up short, and the pain was paralyzing. Monkey Face Guy beat me. I was devastated. Literally crushed. The twelve-year-olds were pissed and upset, but the loss buried me, and it was tough to climb out of. Humiliated and stung, I had diarrhea for three days. When you talk as much shit as I do and you can't back it up, it stings. It stings fucking bad. And when the dust settles and there are no more quick-witted comebacks or excuses to give, you're just a looooooser. It's a tough pill to swallow. Being silenced is deadly for a person like me, who was born and bred for popping shit.

I realized with that loss that a gorilla can win a fantasy football league. It also hit me that the highs and lows I felt from this ridiculously silly game are ridiculous, too. Ultimately, I had no control over this shit. It's a real fucking fantasy.

Regardless of the fact that the DeLight came up short, I have to say that at forty-five years old, I found a new passion in life. I fucking love fantasy football. The competition, the winning, and the losing are all fantastic. But no matter what the results are, nothing beats the high-level shit-talking. I understand now, and it makes perfect sense, why millions of people—friends, family, men, and women—all love it. If you're not a degenerate professional gambler and you're playing fantasy for small stakes and complete shit-talking rights, it's one of the greatest feelings in the world whether you win or lose, like *Matt*.

Twenty-Second Time-Out: Hamilton, *the Musical That's Not Hip-Hop*

We're going to take a twenty-second time-out to get a non-sports-related issue off my chest. I haven't seen the Broadway play *Hamilton*, and there's a great chance I'm never going to see it. I'm not mad at its success, and I'm definitely not mad at Lin-Manuel for breaking barriers and shattering box office records and doing his thing. Go get yours, my man. But I have listened to the soundtrack many times, and we need to get clear on one very simple thing: *Hamilton* is not hip-hop, and it's not rap. Just because the shit rhymes doesn't mean it's rap music, so sooner rather than later, let's stop the madness, please. Nobody was calling Dr. Seuss rap, and that motherfucker rhymed twenty-four hours a day. It's rhyming, not rapping. *Hamilton* is musical theater, not a hip-hop musical.

No one is calling me up saying, "Mike, you need to check out this founding father discovery of America Wu Tang–type shit. I haven't heard anything this sick since Eric B. and Rakim dropped *Paid in Full*." None of my friends are asking me if I've heard that sick new track about Alexander Hamilton and his girl when they first settled in America. Nobody is bumping *Hamilton* before they go out partying with their homeboys for the night. This is not the hip-hop get-hyped anthem album of the year we're talking about. There's no Hammy Ham mixtape coming out soon, and I've never seen a crew of youngsters rocking any *Hamilton* songs while playing ball in the park. You know why that not happening? 'Cause it's not hip-hop and it's just not funky.

Like I said, I'm happy for Lin-Manuel; I love to see any artist make a hit. I love that your music gets people crazy on the Bar Mitzvah circuit and country club barbecues, but Fat Joe ain't coming in on the remix vocal sessions, and my man DJ Premier ain't doing a mashup. Kanye West is not letting you open for him on the 2018 I Ain't Crazy Tour either. You're not getting Outkast to spit on the *Hamilton* mixtape, part 6, just for the love of the game. Kids up in the Bronx are not blaring the shit in their car while kickin' it to the girls on Fordham Road.

When you see athletes in the locker room, lacing up their shoes with their headphones on, guess what they're not listening to: *Hamilton*. Kevin Durant is not getting ready to take on the Cavaliers in the Finals by playing a song about Alexander Hamilton convincing France to join the Revolution. Nobody is getting game-ready to stop Kyrie Irving listening to tracks about joining the Continental Army. Sorry.

And my man Lin, can you please stop freestyling everywhere you go? Come on, man. Every show you're on, there's another freestyle. I get it. I know the tricks. That shit is not new. That Mother Goose bullshit sounds prewritten anyway. Coming out on *The Ellen Show* rhyming *Ellen* with *yellin'* and *sellin'* and *melon*? Enough is enough. *Hamilton* is not hip-hop.

And don't get me started on Broadway in general. I grew up around there. It's overpriced, and the theaters don't have any legroom. You want to pay four hundred bucks for a seat in a theater where your knees bang against the back of the seat in front of you? Fuck that, I'd rather fly in a middle seat in coach on United Airlines, fight a flight attendant, and go on vacation to Detroit for the same price. So yeah, *Hamilton* is straight *South Pacific* musical theater; it's not bumping, it's not banging, and it's not boom bap. It's not hip-hop.

That's my father, my older brother Eric, and our gigantic football at John Jay Park in NYC. If those child-leashing devices had been around in the Seventies, my dad would have been well within his rights to use one on me.

Catching Punts

When I look back, I realize that my father was really good at sports. He wasn't Bo Jackson or anything, but he grew up like most boys in NYC playing stickball in the streets, and legend has it that he even broke a kid's leg playing football when he was twelve. Dad played tennis a few times a week until he was seventy-eight, when he finally had to hang up the racket due to a back injury. No bullshit: he was known at the Manhattan Tennis Club as a player with "museum quality" strokes. He had a stunning one-handed backhand and looked amazing playing the game.

But beyond his talent on the clay courts, my dad had an incredible ability to punt a football. I know it's very specific and not something altogether useful when you have no plans for using it, but as sports-fanatic kids, my brother Eric and I loved it. We would go to John Jay Park on East Seventy-Seventh Street every weekend and watch my father punt the shit out of a regulation football from one end of the park to the other until he was warmed up, and then he would punt it right over the fence at John Jay. I'm pretty sure 99.95 percent of the people reading this book have never been to John Jay Park, so let me lay it out for you. Imagine a standard NYC sports park with a chalk-painted softball diamond on concrete and four single basketball hoops in a square. It's about a sixty-yard-by-sixty-yard area.

My father wears glasses, still has some curly hair left, and sports a prominent Jewish nose that was broken many times throughout the years from sports and being in the army. At six foot one and probably around 210 pounds during his punting prime, he was basically a giant version of your prototypical New York Jewish man. A gigantic Woody Allen with a bit of Larry David. He will be so pissed about the Woody and Larry David comparison, but sometimes the truth hurts, Pops.

Sorry. At least I'm telling the world about your athletic prowess.

As a kid watching my pops punt the football over and over sky-high into the air and watching the excitement and admiration of all the other kids in the park, I felt special. It sounded like a rocket launch when he made contact with the ball. *Boom!* I have to mention he was crushing the ball while wearing jeans or corduroy pants. One time when he was punting in Central Park in 1968, a scout for the Philadelphia Eagles approached him and offered him a tryout for the team. That's a fact. My father was a punting beast, and how he developed that gift, we have no idea. It's like Dirk Diggler says in *Boogie Nights*: "Everybody is born with a gift." Dirk's gift was a giant loaf, and David Rapaport's gift was a superhuman leg.

The thing that was so crazy about the punts at John Jay was that rarely would anybody ever catch the football when it came down. Most of the kids were six to ten years old, and a football that sounds like a gun being shot when it's kicked coming down full speed at you is scary as shit. It takes a bunch of attempts to get it, and the crowd of kids was always around eight to twelve deep, so you didn't have many chances.

Luckily, I had an in with this Jewish punting machine. One Sunday morning in 1977, my dad and I went to the park early on a misty morning. The park was totally empty. Ya snooze, ya lose.

We threw the ball around first, and then my dad started warming up the golden leg. He began with short punts, maybe twenty to thirty yards, and then medium ones, around forty to forty-five, and then he started launching those bad boys in the sky. Every time the ball hit the ground, it would bounce ten feet back in the air and wobble off. I'd chase it down, close the distance between me and my dad, and throw the ball back to him.

On one of the next punts, for some reason and without discussion, my dad launched a medium-length rocket into the air. It went crazy high up and thirty-five yards deep, and I got under it. I don't have a great memory, but I will never forget this moment: I stood under the ball as it came down, cradled my arms, shut my eyes, and waited for it. And out of the fucking blue—*Wham!*—the ball hit me in the chest and rocked me dead onto the concrete, knocking the wind out of me. My father ran over and said, "Michael, are you okay?" I said, "Yeah, I'm good, I think I can catch it. Can you do it again?"

He walked back, and all of a sudden, I remember thinking to myself, I'm gonna catch this ball, I know I can catch this ball. "Do a high one, Dad, I'm gonna catch it," I said, and he did.

Boom! He kicked the crap out of the ball one more time. It had a thunder blast when it connected with his foot. I watched it go all the way up, pushed my sleeves up, ran a few steps back, got right under this giant rubber Wilson, and, I shit you not, caught the damn ball. It knocked me down again, and my legs swung back over my head, and I remember saying, "I got it, Dad, I got it!" My father ran over to me and said, "Holy shit, how did you do that?" He scooped me off the ground and kept saying "Holy shit, how did you catch that?" It was a huge deal for both of us. Nobody ever caught my dad's punts, but on that day, I finally did. My father still tells me to this day: "I can't believe you caught that damn football when you were that young."

LaVar Can't Ball!!!

LaVar Ball, you're acting like the next Octomom or Mama June, bro. You're on some Dance Mom, Housewife, Honey Boo Boo shit. I don't know where you came from or where you're headed, but the shit you're talking needs to stop. You need to get the family together and sort this out. Pull up the chairs, gather round the living room, get the boys all in one room, and talk through it. I don't even know where you came from, but it's time to pump the big baller brakes.

First off, let me be clear: those Ball kids can ball for real. That's obvious, and I respect their game and wish them well, but in my opinion, LaVar, you're making it worse for them with every comment that comes out of your mouth. Some of the shit you say is next-level out there, and it has to be for effect, right? Like you're going for that "Don King in his prime" effect. Right? You say you can beat Michael Jordan in a game of one-on-one? You are sounding crazy on the yard, LaVar. I don't give a damn if Jordan gained forty more pounds and lived on Big Macs: you couldn't beat Michael Jordan, Michael Jackson, Mike Tyson, Michael Bublé, or Michael Keaton—who, by the way, gets my vote as best Batman yet—in a game of one-on-one, Horse, Pig, or 21. You're lost, Duke. You're saying shit that crazy people say, and it's not cute. You said your oldest son is better than Steph Curry right now. I'm letting you know he's not better than Steph, Dell, and, until he proves it, Baby Riley Curry. To quote the great American poet O'Shea Jackson, "Chickity check yourself before you wreck yourself," LaVar.

Talking about how you can beat Michael Jordan. Child, please. The one and only video available of you playing ball looks like you hired a casting director to line up the players against you. They looked like a gang of seven-year-olds too scared to guard you, and you still weren't shit. You were looking real clumsy out there, LaVar. You averaged two motherfucking points a game in college. Take it down a notch.

You are talking reckless. After your son Lonzo's UCLA team got bounced from the 2017 NCAA Tournament, where he got outplayed and out-"Balled" by Kentucky kids, you said, "A team can't win an NCAA Championship with three slow white players"? Really? What about two black guys, a couple of Europeans, and a seven-foot-three Asian phenom? Check Villanova's roster from 2016. Take a close look, my man. They were like the cast of *Friends* doing a cameo on *Empire*.

You came out with the Big Baller Brand sneaker that costs $495 and looks like a snowshoe fucked a flip-flop. What the fuck kind of hokey-pokey shit are you trying to sell? You're talking that three-card-monte, double-talk bullshit. You won't even tell people how much it costs to make those overpriced skips. You know what skips are, right, LaVar? Skips are Payless knockoff versions of the real thing. LaVar, you're playing yourself out here. Talking about the sneaker is for the culture. What culture are those $495 fugazi-ass Nikes for? You're faking jacks out here, LaVar. Those sneakers aren't for the basketball culture, street culture, or the St. Tropez yacht culture. And your Big Baller Brand has a sandal for $220 that doesn't even exist? A few days after you started selling this foolishness, you were photographed wearing Adidas? GTFOH with this shit.

Believe me, my sources let me know that there are players in the NBA just waiting for your kid to get into the league so they can welcome him with open arms and pick-and-rolls to put him on his ass because of your antics.

Lonzo might have to have an "apology from my dad" press conference before he even starts playing, because there are going to be so many players ready to check him on the court it's going to get uncomfortable. Your son might be moving back to his old bedroom after LeBron busts him with a 275-pound elbow. And I like your kids. This isn't about them. I think they can play for real. I wish them the best. I'm a father. I would never wish anyone's kids ill. I don't want your son to stop having fun playing basketball because his life turned into a media circus before he was twenty-one. I want him to shine out there. But you've got to reel it in. You are going to make your kids have to fight your battles. Instead of people talking about what Lonzo can do, they are talking about what he can't do. A lot of people want to see him fail because of YOU. Is that what real Big Ballers do?

That Big Baller bullshit looks like you robbed the tour bus of the 1984 Fresh Festival, then knocked over a Nineties haberdashery where Arrested Development worked. Give my man Speech back his gear. Who the hell is going to wear Kool Moe Dee's sweatshirt in 2018? Big Daddy Kane wants his video clothes back, and he told me that to my face. I don't get it. The shit looks stuffy and uncomfortable, and I know that's not Beefy-T you're working with, so give the Fu Schnickens their shit back and tell Special Ed you're sorry. I think I also saw a Big Baller onesie, and that just hurt my heart. Plus, it all looks hot as hell, like temperature wise, like the material is made out of winter blankets. Are you making blanket T-shirts? That's a fair question. I saw you wearing one of your own T-shirts with an additional undershirt to prevent public sweats. I saw it. Then I saw you show up on TV trying to look legitimate rocking an off-the-rack suit. Come on, man! Real Big Ballers only wear custom-made shit. LaVar, take a chill pill.

I know what it is. I think you really want that reality-show life. You ready for your close-up, LaVar? You're so obnoxious, Magic Johnson compared you to Kris Kardashian, and Magic never disrespects anyone publicly. You're acting like you really want a VH1 show. I do know some people at Bravo TV, and I could make a call for you, but while you may think you're camera ready, I don't think you know your lines. Think it through and hold your head, Big Baller, before you wind up on the E! Channel's next episode of *Where Are They Now?*

The Magic of Magic

Magic Johnson was one of my favorite players growing up, straight up, no doubt about it. I was all about Magic. Six nine, point guard, handling the ball like a magician, and changing the entire idea of what it was to run the point. No one saw the court better, no one was a better leader on the floor, the no-look pass followed by a smile? Are you kidding me? We don't need to go into the stats and the titles and all that. That would only take away from what I felt about him.

Everything about Magic's style on and off the court I loved. I would imitate his walk, mimic his run, and smile for no reason while playing hoops. I'd be in the house slow walking through the living room with that shoulder shake and the short strides with a dash of being pigeon-toed. I wanted to be like Magic, move like Magic, and play like Magic. Who didn't? I would pull my socks up past my calves like he did, even though my calf didn't have the muscle to hold the sock up. And when I got older and caught a glimpse of what Magic was like in life, I was even more impressed. I've never seen anyone fit their name better. The irony was that they gave him that nickname for his playing, not because they knew how magical he was as a person.

I went to his basketball camp in Southern California, where three hundred kids came from all over the country to learn the game. Kids from Detroit, Texas, Florida, Alabama, and New York were all there. It was an amazing mix. And it was all basketball all day. We would start the morning out with old-school calisthenics: touching our toes, doing jumping jacks, push-ups, sit-ups, and all the basics. We looked like a bunch of kids in army boot camp. But we took it seriously, and the competition was real. Kids from Detroit had that same attitude as the New Yorkers, the kids from Alabama looked like they grew up pushing lawn mowers across an acre of lawn, and the Texans were on some quiet, confident shit.

Every day, we'd break off into teams and scrimmage. Those games were intense because Magic was watching, and everyone wanted to be great in front of him. He was walking around the courts, studying us, checking us out, just kind of nodding his head with that slow, cool walk. Some days he had friends like Isiah Thomas and Mark Aguirre come by, which just added to the pressure. I wanted to impress him any time I thought he was looking. If I was in the game and I was on D and I saw Magic looking over, I kicked it into high gear. One of my favorite ballplayers of all time is going watch me play D? You better believe I'm moving my feet faster than they've ever moved and I'm keeping my guy in check. "Let's go, Texas, let's see what you got." My giant pale feet never moved so fast. Every time I touched the ball, I was trying to do that Magic dribble: the high dribble while looking around and smiling. I wasn't even a guard, but I was tall and wanted Magic to think I had handles. Of course, when you dribble high, look around, and smile at fourteen years old, you lose the ball, which happened often. But Magic saw what I was going for.

We'd finish the day with basic drills: shooting, passing, and ball handling. We looked like the Globetrotters when they would go behind their backs and pass to the guy to the right while looking left. Some of the kids noticed I was imitating Magic all the time. One of them asked, "Mike, why are you walking like you're sore and tired already? You haven't done anything yet." I told him it's just how I walk. The truth is there was nothing in my game that was reminiscent of Magic's, except the excitement and love of basketball and the fact that he was tall when he was fourteen.

The most exciting part about camp for me was the day we each got to take our picture with Magic. Every single kid at camp got in line. There were literally three hundred kids waiting to get their picture taken. Just a long-ass line of sweaty strangers in short shorts and tank tops waiting to meet the Magic man. And then it hit me: Magic Johnson is going to wait for every single kid to come up and take their picture? This could take hours. And it did, but he was patient. I mean beyond patient. Not only was he patient, he seemed like he was enjoying it. Magic genuinely appreciated the fact that these kids came to *his* camp. He had a real "moment" with every single kid who stepped up. This went on for three hours, and he never complained, he never even said "Hurry up." He was like Santa Claus at a mall. This was when I realized, "Okay, this isn't just the greatest player in the world, this might be *the greatest person in the world*."

He could have done a group photo and called it a day. He could have split us into two groups, but he didn't. He took a picture with every single kid and made them feel special for that moment. Then it was my turn. I stepped up. I was nervous, but I was ready. I had my socks pulled, set my pigeon toes right, leaned over, and walked up slow. He asked me where I was from. I told him New York, and Magic said right away, "Why don't you have Bernard King socks on?" I said, "You're my favorite." He smiled and gave me quick high five, and we took the picture.

Magic and me in 1984. Please note the socks, and I was even wearing Laker shorts. I'm not just saying this, but when I was around Magic, there was a feeling that he was touched by God or an angel. He had another level of energy. This man was from another dimension. I got some of that Magic dust on me after the picture, and I was set. Camp was amazing, and it only solidified how much I loved the man.

When Magic announced he had HIV and was retiring from basketball, it felt like I got kicked in the gut. Like the rest of the world, I was devastated. Forget retiring from basketball; I was afraid Magic was going to die. We didn't know that much about HIV and AIDS back then, so in my mind it was a death sentence. I thought I was watching Magic talk for the last time. I was never going to see Magic again. I didn't know what was going to happen. I was crying on my couch in my $325-a-month Hollywood apartment watching him on TV. He was standing behind the podium and telling the world he had HIV and that he was retiring from the Lakers. What the hell was happening? I felt powerless and crushed. But there was one thing that stuck out to me while watching this unfold. I noticed the people around Magic wiping their tears and scared to death, heads down on the table, and the only one that was holding it together with his head up was Magic! He had grace and dignity and poise, exactly like he had on the court. He told us he was going to fight this, and he did. By the end of the conference, I was still stunned, but I thought if anyone could handle this, it was Magic. Obviously, like most of the country, it took me some time to adjust to the game without Magic, and it was always on my mind. My favorite player, my favorite person, was taking a long hiatus from the game he loved.

I saw Magic in a restaurant not too long ago, and once again, just like Santa, people were coming up to him one at a time wanting to take a picture. Kids, adults, elderly people with dogs in tow all headed over to his table to have their moment. It was like a scene from a church where people come up on stage with ailments looking to be saved. Magic was saving the entire restaurant. He didn't deny anyone. There were a few people I might have sent back. One dude called him Kareem, and Magic shook his hand and took a picture. He didn't just say hello either. He stood up, shook their hand, said something cool and inspiring, then sat back down to eat. But as soon as he picked up his fork, another person showed up at the table. His turkey chopped salad was getting soggy, and no one cared. It looked crazy over there.

He had to be tired. Magic is six foot nine, 265 pounds, and he's standing up and sitting down every forty-five seconds, and every single exchange was 100 percent genuine. I was thinking, Yo, give him a break or pull up a seat, his knees are killing him. Those are championship knees that spent years running full speed. But he kept greeting them. Up and down, like a sore giant, smiling, shaking a hand, kissing a baby, petting a dog, saying something nice. I was just taking notes. I started thinking about myself and how I am when I meet people. I could be better. Don't get me wrong: I'm always gracious with fans—I love fans—but I don't remember the last time I stood up to shake a hand. I have a grumpy side, and I don't love standing. I do most things seated, plus I'm a clean freak. I'm not shaking a hand if it's flu season. Magic doesn't give a shit about flu season. When it was over, he finally got some peace and dove back into his meal, and I looked over at him, and right then it hit me: Of course we all love Magic, but maybe not as much as Magic loves us.

The Beautiful Audacity of Muggsy Bogues

Why the fuck isn't Muggsy Bogues giving daily TED Talks? Why is he not on the list of speakers at your motivational seminars? Why is Muggsy Bogues not the next Tony Robbins or Wayne Dyer or that whacked-out new-age mullet-having bleached-toothed weirdo Joel Osteen? I'll listen to anything Muggsy has to say forever. Why? Because he's five-foot-fucking-three and he played almost fifteen years in the NBA among the giants! Of course you're going to listen to Tony Robbins. He's eight feet tall with baseball glove hands and a head that looks like it was made on Halloween! You're scared to *not* listen to him. When he points at you, you shit yourself quickly, then cry. I want to hear what Muggsy Bogues has to say. Do you have any idea of the kind of mind-set someone like that must have? This is someone who looked in the mirror his whole life and saw himself as a Beast. I can only imagine the conversations he was having in grade school when they tried to lock him into typical short-status roles.

Teacher: Tyrone, we're going to have you playing a member of the Lollipop Guild for *The Wizard of Oz* Friday. Isn't that great?

Muggsy: Nah, I'm playing the Lion.

Teacher: Oh, we don't have a lion suit for you.

Muggsy: Yeah, I don't need a suit. I'm actually a motherfucking lion.

Teacher: We don't need to curse, Tyrone.

Muggsy: Just call me Muggsy.

Teacher: Okay, well, the Lollipop Guild players are a fun role, Muggsy.

Muggsy: I don't even know what the fuck you're saying right now. I'm playing the Lion, and afterward I might eat a lollipop if I'm hungry.

Teacher: Okay, well, we have the role of Toto open.

Muggsy: The fuck did you say?

Teacher: In our version, Toto has lines.

Muggsy: In my version, I eat dogs. I'm the Lion, or I'm gonna burn the play down.

Teacher: Someone's going to get detention if they keep up this attitude.

Muggsy: All good—I love detention; it's where I do my push-ups and box jumps and daydream about playing pro basketball.

Teacher: You want me to notify your parents, young man?

Muggsy: Go ahead. They know I'm a lion. They tell me every day, "You're a lion and a beast."

Teacher: I don't understand.

Muggsy: I figured you wouldn't. Now, when are rehearsals? I'm gonna work on my roar.

I met Muggsy at a Knicks game in 2015. I introduced myself to him, then said these exact words: "Yo, Muggsy, I know you're a motherfucker. You're a bad motherfucker 'cause to do what you did in the league is no joke, my man." When I was next to him, I could feel the man's presence. And even though I have more than fifty pounds and a foot in height on him, I can guarantee that Muggsy Bogues could whoop my ass. He was giving off some sort of Luke Cage meets Shaft–type of vibe. Like if I said the wrong thing, he would whip around and punch me in the thigh and fuck my whole body up.

I've met a lot of athletes, but meeting Muggsy was something I'll never forget.

Muggsy Bogues needs to be on a mental toughness speaking tour that lets anyone know that with the right amount of "fuck what you heard, you can't tell me shit," you, too, can be anything you want. Muggsy Bogues is on some Bobby Fischer, Steve Jobs, Richard Branson, "let's go to Mars for a picnic on a Thursday"–type of shit. Do you realize what kind of forward-thinking imagination and true-blue "fuck the world, don't ask me for shit" mentality you have to have to be five foot three, 135 pounds, and named Tyrone to play in the NBA? Muggsy didn't just defy logic; he defied physics.

Give Muggsy a microphone and a speaking tour schedule and let me know where he is going to be, because I need to hear what he has to say. Who the hell knows what I'll do after listening to motivational Muggsy for an hour? I might run right out of the place from LA to New York because I think I can and I know I can. I might train only underhanded set shots in my driveway and try out for the NBA next year. Who the fuck knows what I'll do? And why the fuck isn't that actor Peter Dinklage not talking about Muggsy in all of his interviews? They're like two inches apart in size and both killing it in their fields. One is slaying giants on a TV show, and the other one slayed them in real life.

People say Michael Jordan should replace Jerry West as the NBA logo? Fuck no. It should be Muggsy Bogues. Put Muggsy on the shirt—I don't care if it's a life-size iron-on. He deserves it. Tyrone "Muggsy" Bogues needs to be sharing his secrets with the world so Tony Robbins can quit bullying everyone into being motivated. Muggsy's thoughts should be recorded for future generations so people who are told that they don't have a shot can listen to him and then conquer their fears. There's racism, there's sexism, and there's classism in this country, but Tyrone "Muggsy" Bogues overcame itty-bitty-ism to be what I think is one of the greatest minds in professional sports history.

Geno, Go Get Your Shine Box, Geno

Let me start by saying I love women's basketball. I don't have a problem with women's basketball at all. Fuck it, I've played women's basketball. I get right in. I don't shy away from competition. I've had my ass busted by women in basketball. Let's get that straight out the gate. I've played in celebrity games with Sue Bird, Skylar Diggins, and Lisa Leslie and a bunch of others, and I know where I stand. I have the utmost respect for women who play ball. And I have mad respect for the University of Connecticut's fantastic women's basketball team, but they're straight demolishing teams and it's getting ridiculous. Now, again, I don't have a problem with the talented young women on that team. But I have a real problem with the coach. Yeah. I got a real fuckin' problem.

That's right. Geno Arena, Orama, Oreantique, Aubama, or however the fuck you say your last name. I have a problem, and I think a few others might as well, but they're too damned scared to talk about it. Guess who's not scared? Michael Rapaport, the Gringo Mandingo, a.k.a. Milk, a.k.a. White Mike. That's right, Geno. The shit is out of balance.

You've won one hundred games in a row, and fifty-six of them you won by 40 points or more. Geno, when is enough enough?

You look like a fuckin' girl bully. How about I go get some real girl bully goons from Brownsville, Brooklyn. Some girls who eat fuckin' hoop dreams for breakfast. Huh? How about I drive a bus around and collect a gang of girls to bully your team? Or maybe they just do a little shove job on you personally, Geno. Would that be fun for you? What I really want to know is why the hell you haven't moved on. You conquered women's college hoops, now get on with it. Grab your balls and coach somewhere else—anywhere else. Let's go. It's time to step it up.

When will you finally look around the arena and think, "Maybe it's time to take my talents elsewhere? I've done everything I can in this league. I've shit on every program in our division and around the country, and I think I need a real challenge in my life." Maybe, just maybe, it's time to play with the big girls in the WNBA. Or maybe, just maybe, it's time to play with some men! You ever think about that? You want to go down as one of the great coaches of all time? Your record might get you a meeting, but you don't get a seat at the table. Nope. Sorry. You don't sit with the Vince Lombardis, Bobby Knights, Phil Jacksons, Popovichs, or the Bill Belichicks, and if you see the ghost of John Wooden, get him some damn water, 'cause the man's soul is thirsty from years and years of hard-fought competition and constantly challenging himself. You're embarrassing teams, Geno, and that's not what the game is about. That's not what life is about. You don't get a seat at the Big Boy table, Auramimi. You walk into that room and you try to take a seat, and it's gonna kinda feel like a scene straight out of *Goodfellas*. And you ain't Joe Pesci, my friend. You're Spider. Remember Spider? He was the kid Joe Pesci's character shot in the foot for not getting his drink order right. Let me spell it out for you. I know a thing or two about scenes.

INT. BACK ROOM—ITALIAN RESTAURANT—NIGHT

Geno Aureemariosta walks in; others take notice. Around the table sit the great coaches of the past and present: Bobby Knight, Vince Lombardi, Phil Jackson, Gregg Popovich, Bill Belichick, and John Wooden. Geno takes a seat. The others look on with disdain. Stunned, even.

Popovich: Hey, fellas, look, it's Geno Amorosa. Hey, what's the good word, Geno, what team you just finish embarrassing this week?

Geno: Hey, guys. We just beat Central Florida by fifty-five, and Tulsa the night before by sixty. Shit, I'm exhausted from all the ass kicking. We got any beers?

Bobby Knight: As a matter of fact, we do. Why don't you head to the fridge and fetch me and Mr. Lombardi a couple of cold ones?

Geno: You're funny.

Bobby Knight: Funny? How the fuck am I funny? What the fuck is so funny about me? Funny like a clown? Do I amuse you, Eugene?

Geno: No, I was just saying you're funny. I mean, you tell me to get you beers and all, and I'm blowing teams out left and right; you know, I just thought that was funny.

Coach Lombardi: You're blowing out girls, is that right?

Geno: Yes, Vince.

Coach Lombardi: It's Mr. Lombardi.

Geno: Sorry about that, Mr. Lombardi.

Bobby Knight: You ever think about maybe coaching men, Auremini?

Geno: Nah—I mean, I got a good thing going, ya know? It's Auriemma.

Bobby Knight: You think you got a good thing going, huh? I split wins with Purdue in '87 in what we call a goddamn rivalry and then went on to win the title that year. No blowouts. We fought hard. I caught a stress hernia in 1987. I haven't been the same since.

Popovich slams his hand down on the table hard. Geno goes wide-eyed, scared of what might come next.

Popovich: You're on easy street, Geno. I've seen the freakin' Lakers seven times in the playoffs in my life. You know what that feels like? Huh? You know what the fuck it feels like to NOT know what the hell is going to happen in a game? You don't think challenging yourself makes any sense!

Geno: I mean, we're really killing these teams, and I like the feeling of it—and, you know, we did just lose for the first time to Mississippi State during the tournament—

Bobby Knight: Thank fucking goodness!

Geno: Well, I was trying to tell you guys—

Bobby Knight: You trying to impress us with all that killing you're doing, Geno? You a killer?

Phil Jackson: My shoulder's got a fuckin' knot! Come rub it out, will ya, Geno? I got a knot from sitting too long during meditation and thinking about the Jordan Rules that the goddamn Detroit Pistons implemented when they took my title in 1989! Who's got the Epsom salts?

Popovich: Try to relax, Phil. Geno, you heard him. He's got a meditation knot, now get at it.

Geno: I don't think I really—

Belichick: Rub the fuckin' muscle, Geno. Shit! Now look what happened over here.

Belichick spills hot sauce on his ripped hoodie. No one moves. Knight pipes up.

Bobby Knight: Now this. The man spilled on his favorite sweatshirt, and Phil's all knotted out. Bust through the knot, Geno, will ya? You do massage, don't you, Geno?

Geno: No, no, I don't really do massages.

Bobby Knight: Oh no, you don't do massages? You blow out women's basketball teams by fifty, that's what you do? You win one hundred games in a row and no one comes close to beating you and you're happy about that?

Coach Lombardi: He's happy with that. Lifetime I'm 105 to 35 and 6. I know what it is to lose. Not much, but I know. It made me strong. *[Coughs.]* Excuse me.

Bobby Knight gets up from the table and hurls a metal chair against the wall.

Bobby Knight: See what the fuck I do now?

Coach Lombardi: The man's angry.

Geno: Well, I mean—

Belichick: Get my sweatshirt, Geno. You're embarrassing me. You never even had to make a comeback. You ever watch the Super Bowl, Geno? It's a big game played by men.

Geno: Come on, Coach, of course—

Belichick: Grab my hoodie before you give Phil a rubdown.

Geno: Come on, guys, I was just trying to sit down and have a drink and talk shop.

Phil Jackson: Roll me a joint and rub my toe, too! The shit hurts.

Geno: Guys.

Bobby Knight: Don't "guys" us. Step up your level of competition, Geno. You're not earning. Put a Purdue in your life. Put a Kentucky in your world. A team that challenges you game after game, season after season. Earn it.

Coach Lombardi: Man needs to earn.

Popovich: You disgust me right now, Eugene.

Bobby Knight: Be a man, Geno.

Phil Jackson: Step it up.

Coach Lombardi: You're such a winner, huh? Well, it's time to take your talents elsewhere, Aureemama.

Geno: It's Auriemma.

ALL AT ONCE: The fuck cares what it is?

Geno: But, fellas, I thought we were all friends.

Popovich: You thought wrong, fuck nose. Leave the women alone, Geno.

Bobby Knight: It's embarrassing for all of us.

Coach Lombardi: The streets are talking.

Geno: I'll work on it. Why are you breakin' my balls?

Bobby Knight: Geno, if I was breakin' your balls, I'd tell ya to go get your fucking shine box.

One by one the coaches slowly get up from the table, leaving Geno to contemplate his future alone. Geno hangs his head while Lombardi's soul dissipates into the thin air, Phil gets up with a cane, Bobby Knight mumbles something under his breath about the Republican party and hurries out, Popovich takes a last swig of his beer and heads for the door, and Belichick keeps scrubbing the stain from his weathered hoodie.

FADE OUT

You made it through that scene the same way you make it through every one of your seasons, Geno: unscathed. But unscathed is no way to go through life, my man. If you expect your players to step up to the challenges they face every day on and off the court, then maybe you need to challenge yourself in another endeavor, Geno, and if that's not something you're willing to do, then, seriously, go get your shine box and . . . I'm kidding, Geno, I'm kidding. Take a leap of faith, man. The worst that can happen is you win a few games by two points and not fifty. Or maybe your team goes on a four-game losing streak. It happens to the best of them. Bouncing back is part of the process. It doesn't feel as bad as you might think, Geno.

Fuck Spin Class

My wife actually looks forward to working out every day. She's one of those people who can wake up at 5:30 a.m. sharp with a smile on her face, ready to seize the moment. She hops straight out of bed and is at a workout class before I've even hit the snooze button a second time. She's an animal with it.

Bae's always pushing me to stay in shape, too, and work out with her, so I've been going along and trying to find a class that doesn't suck. She's worth it. First, it was spin class. It didn't work out because of the fact that I had severe chafing and broke out in a rash within the first three shitty songs the spin leader played. I don't like bike riding in real life, so why the fuck would I enjoy being in a dark room spinning with disco lights and a whacked-out, overly aggressive fake Lance Armstrong screaming at me? The guy had a hit-or-miss playlist that weaved right into twelve god-forsaken minutes of EDM for the momentous "Big Ride" death fest. They actually refer to it as the Big Ride? Well, guess what? We ain't going anywhere on the Big Ride, so cut the bull-shit, pal. We ain't going anywhere. We're spinning in circles like a gang of circus monkeys all looking around to see who's gonna faint first and which of you guys got convinced to show up by your girl, too. Spin wasn't for me, but then my wife got me into cross-fit for a while. Another batch of exercises that have no relevance in life.

I honestly was enjoying cross-fit until I tweaked a hammy doing tire pushes. Tire pushes are when the "cross-fitter," in this instance me, is supposed to flip a three-hundred-pound tire over and over up and down the gym. It's some real gooned-out ultra-man-strength shit you saw thirty years ago on *Wide World of Sports*, but it was only done by giant Swedish monsters and Russian assassins who made side money by lifting cars.

That day I was doing great for about three flips, and then being Jewish happened. I fell into the middle of the fucking tire headfirst and wound up getting rescued by two rough and rugged cross-training ladies who thought the whole thing was hilarious. I suffered aloud making real fucked-up noises with my head in the tire. It was like a whine that echoed in the tire. I didn't know if anyone heard me. It was lonely inside that tire. I was injured, and I couldn't have been more Jewy and broken. It was some Larry David–type shit for real. I cut my forehead, and my left hamstring had no feeling. I thought I snapped it. I needed to take a cross vacation for a while. My girl was embarrassed, and the people she knew looked at her like they were saying, "He's really nice, but he's not built for this shit." The trainer put me on injured reserve for ten days so I could heal up and get my head straight.

During my cross-fit sabbatical, I started questioning how I got injured in the first place. Did I overthrow the tire? Were my legs too long to bend and lift? Was this shit really made for shorter people who didn't have to bend so far to reach the tire? Chuck, my cross-fit guru and cock diesel-ed hipster trainer convinced me that the exercises were basic and functional and there was no reason for me to fall headfirst into a tire that was already on the ground. I started thinking about the word *functional.* Chuck loved that fucking word. Functional? How functional is flipping a three-hundred-pound tire down the road? It's 2017 right now. They have tow trucks and all sorts of services that can help with your runaway truck tire. Functional, my ass. Do I own a truck scrapyard? When the fuck would I ever need to use this skill? I don't live on a farm. The tractor I don't own is never breaking down in the middle of the cornfields that I've never seen. There's nothing functional about a forty-seven-year-old man doing tire flips in a Silver Lake cross-fit gym with a gang of dudes with beards and no body fat.

My next "Fuck Cross-Fit, It's Not for Me" epiphany hit me during my injury break while looking at my severely callused hands. They looked like I had spent years building skyscrapers and used sandpaper for lotion. I didn't wear gloves for a little while, and I regret it. The Cross-Fit Community, which I love and respect, will never admit this publicly, but they look down on people wearing gloves when they work out. Well, I have the hands of a fucking ballerina, and I always have. They're soft, and I'm proud of it. These hands ain't made for power lifting. My hands are big, soft, and fragile and wanted to play piano at the same time I was playing ball. I need gloves to protect these puppies, but out of respect I went gloveless for a bit. I had been doing pull-ups and motherfucking burpies gloveless for three months, and my hands looked like they had committed heinous crimes. They felt fucked up, too. I was glove shamed every time I asked Chuck for my construction gloves for the thick "no reason to do this either unless I'm climbing down a building during a fire" rope-climbing class.

If you have never done cross-fit, they have lumberjack ropes hanging from the gym ceiling. These are ropes people use for towing boats and holding barges on docks. This is the shit they used before cables were invented and they still had pirates. These shits were on another level of thick. I finally learned to climb the fucking rope sixteen feet up to the ceiling and ring a bell. It was a great feeling, a feeling of accomplishment, a feeling of breaking through to the other side. You know what it also felt like? It felt like I had been tricked and the teacher wanted me dead. What they don't teach you in ropes class is how to come down from the ceiling on a giant deadly rope. The Indian burns I got on my legs on the way down and the bleeding hands that were ripping apart had me crying on the inside like a fucking circus acrobat who fell and tried to act fine about it. I was blank-faced and bleeding out.

What the fuck is functional about being able to climb a rope? They have elevators and stairs and escalators now. Yeah, it's cool and was impressive to Wife-Wife, but you know what else was impressive? My eating eleven slices of Patsy's Pizza the night Larry Johnson hit that four-point play versus the Indiana Pacers in '99. My homeboys couldn't fucking believe what they were seeing. They still talk about me pulling that off without barfing. I had an iron stomach. You know what else is impressive? Sitting happily for seven hours straight during playoff football in one sports bar trying all their different flavors of wings. Why isn't that as impressive? Fuck all this extra hard-core training for events that don't happen in life. Flip a tire, climb a rope, jump up on a box, dangle from the monkey bars? Why don't we do a real functional workout? Why don't I just open and close the car door fifty times? Why don't I pick up a twenty-pound bag of ice forty times to be ready for when the fellas come over to watch games? Why don't I work out my wrists on the barbecue on and off switch in case that day comes? Fuck the nonfunctional functional workout.

I called Chuck the Trainer after the bleeding rope episode and told him I was retiring from cross-fit. He called me a pussy. I told Chuck to take his fucking thirty-five-pound kettle bells and jump into the ocean and let me know how functional that feels, ya prick-lipped function fuck.

Bae was pissed, but luckily, she started to take hot yoga and was thinking about becoming a certified yoga teacher. I was all for it. I wanted to support her, and this was something I could do. No blood, no gloves, no hate. Plus, yoga is something I've practiced over the years and actually like. I'm surprisingly good at it, too. I have a naturally perfect downward dog pose. No bullshit. It's one of those weird things. I could always touch my toes.

Growing up, I was never the best shooter, rebounder, or defensive player, but I was always the best stretcher. Real talk. At Erasmus Hall High School, Coach Bunyon would have me lead the team in pre-practice warm-ups and say wild shit like "Watch Rapaport stretch; he's as flexible as a Honduran hooker on a Sunday." The whole team was confused by Mr. Bunyon's analogies, but I was the best at something, and stretching was it.

I willingly stretch every day, and I'll do it anyplace and any moment I'm feeling a tweak, some tightness, or emotionally unstable. When my kids were eleven and nine, they named me the Street Stretcher because when we would walk around NYC, I would stop on a dime and throw my leg on top of a mailbox to get a nice deep full-leg stretch in. They would be humiliated yet impressed that I could slap my leg on top of a mailbox and go deep midday. I was totally down with my lady going to hot yoga, and I wanted in on the action. This was something I could do.

So, we started going four to five times a week. I loved it. They played dope music in the fifty-minute classes, and I was starting to really get in shape and enjoy myself. Things were going well on all levels. I was long, I was lean, I was limber. My general wingspan was getting wider, and I was breathing deeper. I was even noticing weird shit like when I waved to people, my fingers were more spread out. The yoga was working. My anger spurts were diminishing, and my girl was shocked at how calm I was in restaurants, public spaces, and even on the phone, where I was known to lose it. And then things started to go south.

One day after an extremely hard, sweaty, near-death heat class, I got up to walk out like I usually did, and there were fucking sweat puddles on the floor all over the place like a goddamn rainstorm had happened in the class. I don't do well with other people's sweat in general, but you put buckets of ass and back sweat around the room, and I'm going to lose it. I was hopping around the class like a freakin' lily pad frog looking to get around the water. Everyone in the class was all calm and relaxed and on that "everything is one and everything is part of the same universe and we're all just molecules connected" shit, and I'm thinking, I'm not stepping in homeboy's back-to-ass sweat, and if I do, I'll never do yoga again. The entire purpose was backfiring on me. I didn't want to go back, but of course, Wifey told me I was being a germaphobe and it was so good for me that I had to go back. So, of course, I did. And the shit was fucked up again.

I was in downward dog and the teacher came over and pulled some prison shit on me. He held my hips and started whispering some shit in my ear about me being too tight and that I needed to let my childhood go and drop the pain in my soul. The motherfucker had me in a hip grip with a twist of mind control thrown in. Believe me, I know some of these yoga fucks are on some weird cult control moves. But that's not my point here. This was a man with both hands on me, telling me to let go of all my shit, and he was going to be there for me when it was all over. I didn't like it, I didn't feel right about it, and I left there with a fucking sliver of manhood and swore I wasn't going back. Of course, my lady wasn't having it, and I was back two weeks later for what would be my last class with other people. But this was not my fault either.

The class was going okay, and I was breathing deeply, and my girl was breathing near me and we were all good on a Saturday afternoon, and then Fuckface Von Stretcherberg tells the class that we need to go deep and breathe from our stomachs and let it all go. Well, guess what, kids? When I breathe deep and exhale, sounds are made, and they ain't fucking silent. That's right. I was taught as a young athlete and karate student during my four weeks of karate that when you exhale, you blow it out, and with that blow sometimes comes a sound or a grunt. Well, when I started exhaling, it was coming out somewhere between a "ha" and "ohhhh," and it was purely natural. I wasn't doing it for attention; it's just the way my lungs were kicking out my breath. I felt great, I felt organic, and I felt like it was working. Well, here comes the teacher and tells me, "Michael, I'm sorry, you're disturbing the class." He's telling me this while I'm half upside down and feeling good about myself. I was pissed. This is how I breathe; you want to tell me to go deep and bring it up and exhale, well, this is what you get, my friend. That was it for me. When I got home, my girl told me I actually was disruptive and people were making faces at her since they knew she was with me. Well, guess what, yogis? Have at it. I'm going solo on that ass. I'm done with cultish classes and judgmental techniques, and I now do private yoga all by myself. I make all the loud noises I want, and I don't have to skip over a puddle, and there's no teacher to have his way with me midway through class. Namaste, Bish'es!!!!

Even When We Suck, New York City Is Still the Mecca

New York City is the mecca of basketball, and Madison Square Garden is its crown jewel. I know a lot of you Rapaport pundits from all corners of the world are going to challenge me on this fact, and that's fine. I know you'll tout your city and brag about its great marquees. I know Detroit produced some of the greatest players to ever play the game at the college and pro levels, and you played at the Palace of "Where the Hell Is" Auburn Hills, and, yeah, I know Flint, Michigan, had its heyday when Glen Rice and Jeff Grayer looked like pros in high school. Yes, everyone knows Chicago churned out tons of legends from the parks and the public school system, and people love the United Center and treat it like sacred ground. I've heard it all before. But nothing, *nothing* can touch New York City, and no building can ever touch the World's Most Famous Arena.

The average Rapaport critic (and there are legions of them) will say, "Mike Rap, stop it with the NYC, Madison Square Garden nonsense. The Knicks haven't won shit since 1973, St. John's hasn't been mentionable since Chris Mullin had floppy red hair, and NYC doesn't have any homegrown stars in the NBA." I know all of that. It means nothing. Nada. Zilch.

You can't rewrite history, people. Before the NBA was the big business we know it as today, there was only college basketball to pay attention to, and all the big games and major tournaments happened in New York at Madison Square Garden. Look, I'm not gonna sit here and pretend it doesn't hurt that the Knicks haven't won jack bone since I was three years old. I was actually in a double-legged diaper cast after breaking my leg in the spring of '73 when the Knicks won their last championship. You know how humiliating it was for me to hobble around New York City in a double-legged diaper cast? It fucking sucked.

I was jumping on the bed, fell, and broke my femur. Thank God medical technology has improved, because this casting device was not cool. I didn't even get to go to the parade.

Not winning since '73 is shameful. It hurts bad. I feel it every day when I wake up and look at the posters of Earl "the Pearl"

Monroe I still have hanging on my wall even though I'm pushing fifty. It also hurts that New York City doesn't produce the born-and-bred talent that it used to and isn't sending kids to the NCAA or the NBA like we were once known for. The shit is emotional, and it stings. But life is a big circle and things come back around, my friend. We will rise once again from the streets of New York City and take off like a rocket ship into the stratosphere. I love saying NASA shit like that. We're already making strides. NYC's own Kemba Walker just made his first All-Star Game in 2017 and for now might be the sole rep of the city, and that's okay. Kemba embodies the True-Blue, Boogie-Down-Bronx, Ankle-Breaking Flavor that has influenced the world.

These times are crippling for a guy like me who loves to talk shit and has been perfecting the art since I was thrown out of an NYC public school for it. But knowing the Garden's history and knowing that we're bound to come back gives me real hope, and at this point a little hope is all I'm fucking looking for.

Before the NBA was the gigantic business it is today, with nonstop coverage, statistics filling up every space, and access to star players through social media, the Garden was the place to be. Before Charles, Kenny, and the TNT crew did their thing, people were talking about the Garden as if it was the star. When college hoops was at its height and we were locked in watching NCAA Basketball at its peak, MSG was the epicenter. Please don't make me go all the way back to sold-out Garden appearances by P. T. Barnum and my dude Pickles the Clown to make my point. I think you get it: the Old Garden on Eighth and Fiftieth was the spot, and if you played there, the eyes of the world were watching you. The NBA doesn't get big without New York winning. Period.

I'm no history major, but let me lay it out for you. From '57 through '69, the Boston Celtics won every NBA championship except one. I'm sure that was great for Boston Celtics fans, and it gave some twisted hope even the fans of the Lakers, who lost in the Finals seven times during that period. Unfortunately, the rest of the country didn't give a shit about it. The fact is, the NBA wasn't considered a mainstream attraction until the New York Knicks started winning games, and that, my friends and angry pundits, happened with our 1969–70 Knicks crew.

When that 1970 championship team was organically drafted and traded to make all the pieces fit, they represented NYC and everything about it. Willis Reed, the captain, was only a second-round pick but brought a toughness and work ethic that the city appreciated when he beat up the entire Lakers team in a bench-clearing brawl in 1966. If you have never seen the footage, look it up on YouTube. He beat up the whole team by himself. New Yorkers recognized we had somebody special going to war for us.

Bill Bradley was a star like no other when he got to the Knicks. Women were showing up to the games just to see Dollar Bill on the free-throw line. The hype was nothing like the league had ever seen. He was like a one-man boy band. The closest thing to compare it to was Linsanity. Remember that shit? Fucking Linsanity was some alien-landing shit. Bill Bradley represented that upper-class white Fifth Avenue alien that rounded out our gritty pack of wolves.

The biggest star turned out to be Walt Frazier. Clyde was the first of his kind in pro sports. Every athlete in every sport now comes into the league having already branded themselves and stockpiled endorsements. Walt Frazier and the Clyde image were groundbreaking. He was the first professional athlete to have a sneaker named after him. He was the first to become a mainstream, fully marketable black athlete. That happened because the real-life Mad Men of Madison Avenue were sitting courtside at Knick games watching Frazier emerge, and then they had something special. Clyde was the coolest guy in sports, and maybe the coolest guy to walk the streets of the city. No other player was rockin' canary gold with zebra patterns and a pimped-out brim hat pregame. He played the role of style god on and off the court. They called him Clyde because of the wide-brim Bonnie and Clyde hat that legendary Stick Man Warren Beatty made famous.

We got Dave DeBusschere in the trade from Detroit, and he came in looking like a blue-collar workhorse straight off 8 Mile Road. The City loved him for it. The great Dick Barnett, Cazzie Russell, and the openly Hippie Dippie Smoke-It-If-You-Got-It Phil Jackson were the perfect fit for an NYC-character-driven team. Red Holzman was a tough, street-ball-playing New York City Jew who coached like the city of Brooklyn itself was running through his veins.

That team looked like they played. Every player represented an aspect of New York. They repped the big dreams and harsh realities. The slogan "If you can make it here, you can make it anywhere" was never more apparent than in the lineup and work ethic of the 1970 Knicks. And when they started winning games, it was Madison Square Garden that became the real Broadway show. Fuck *Hamilton*. Nothing was as exciting in 1970 as the Knicks in the Garden.

Celebrities showed up every night: Barbra Streisand, Woody Allen, Bill Cosby, Frank Sinatra, and everyone in between was there. Celebrities didn't go to hoop games before that 1970 championship team. Even the great Laker teams in Los Angeles didn't get the Triple-A-list stars the Knicks got during the 1969–70 season.

The entertainment value of the entire league shot up when the Knicks took the championship. It happened right before our eyes and in dramatic fashion. When a young Marv Albert said,

"Here comes Willis, here comes Willis," as the limping Knicks captain made his way onto the Garden floor and led the Knicks in crushing the Lakers, it was written in stone. The Lakers' original Big 3 of Wilt Chamberlain, Elgin Baylor, and Jerry "the Logo" West had their plans ruined in the Brand-New Garden. The "New Garden" gave new life to the already amazing city.

It's within eyeshot of the Empire State Building and a fifteen-minute walk to Central Park if you go north and to SoHo if you head south. Walk around New York, you'll notice there's an outdoor hoop court within about a mile radius everywhere you go in the five boroughs. Basketball is part of the architectural fabric of New York. That will never go away.

The New Garden opened in 1969 and is the *only* original arena left in the NBA. Although our Knicks haven't won the chip since '73, NBA players, pro fighters, Miley Cyrus, and everybody else knows that when they come to the Garden, this is the same exact building where Clyde had 36 and 19 in game 7 versus the Lakers in 1970, the same roof that Ali and Frazier fought under in 1971, and the same exact seating arrangement that Sinatra performed live to in 1974.

The Boston Garden is gone; the Staples Center is cool but will never have the mystique of the Fabulous Forum. And do I really need to mention other places like the Smoothie King Arena in New Orleans? I don't think so. Madison Square Garden is the last remaining NBA arena with all its history intact. That means everything. Like it or not, the Garden will *always* be the World's Most Famous Arena, and New York City will always be the mecca.

The Irony of Charles Oakley

Of all the lowlights the Knicks have gone through the past few years, the Charles Oakley incident, which I watched on live TV, blew my fucking mind. I couldn't believe what I was seeing, and I damn sure couldn't believe who I was seeing it happen to. I was actually embarrassed to be a New York Knicks fan that day. You don't do Charles Oakley like that. No fucking way. They not only arrested Charles Oakley in Madison Square Garden but the way they handled it afterward was disgusting and against everything we as Knicks fans stand for. That's our dude. They hit him with disorderly conduct and some other bullshit charges, and at the moment of this writing, James Dolan—owner of the Garden, the Knicks, and a billion dollars' worth of other shit—still hasn't dropped the charges. We're talking about Charles Oakley. The same security guards and police officers who grew up in the Tri-State area watching Oakley dive all over the Garden floor for loose balls, set smashing picks, grab rebound after rebound, and protect the players who needed to be protected were now ordered to arrest him? The irony. Oakley went to war for the team he loved representing. Oak was the guy for us, the guy you need on your team. The dude who doesn't do the talking, the dude who does the hard work, and he did it for the last relevant Knicks team you can remember. They physically escorted him to the tunnel, the same tunnel he used to lead the beloved Nineties Knicks team down before they hit the floor. Then, in some sort of bullshit show of force, they put him in a Muay Thai, Krav Maga, Jujitsu arm bar and sat him on the floor. All this was happening on national TV, while the Garden crowd cheered "Oakley, Oakley." It was filthy.

Arresting Charles Oakley in the Garden is like arresting the Pope at the Vatican. He means that much to Knicks fans. He is us. He's what we represent. The hard-nosed, tough-it-out, workmanlike mentality that built New York. And you want to surround him and take him down in his house? Oakley gave us what was real about the city. The real New York shit, not the *Sex and the City*, fashion forward, "SoHo version with a twist of lemon" New York. I'm talking about the motherfuckers who clear your streets, who make sure your garbage gets picked up, who build those skyscrapers you're so proud of. I'm not talking about the man-bun, coffee-shop-hipster, fuck-Brooklyn version that Lena Dunham so gladly portrays on HBO's *Girls*. That ain't New York. That's some elitist, "take off your clothes even when you shouldn't because you read a few books and went to a few art exhibits" bullshit. Charles Oakley is us. Oak repped the heart and soul of New York, and that's how you want to do him? You understand what a guy like that does for your team? Does for your players? You know what it means to have protection on a team, to have that bodyguard on the squad who makes sure you don't get taken advantage of? Every team needs an Oakley. You think Patrick could have been Patrick without knowing Oak had his back? You think Starks didn't get that extra confidence knowing damn well Oakley had straight goon tendencies if he needed them? And don't tell me we already had that with Mason, because as truly bad-ass as Mason was—and we know he was—Oakley was ready to go when it was go time. He's a necessary cog in that machine. That character is needed on every team in every sport.

You don't have Gretzky without McSorley, or Yzerman without Probert. Your stars don't shine without the confidence of knowing they have protection. Why do you think Kobe loved having Ron Artest around? Because he knew damn well if the shit went down, Ron was ready to go and throw for the greater good. The intangible tough-guy shit is real, and it represents the struggle of the people and the work ethic of the everyman. So, when you played Oakley like that, you set the stage for a rebellion, my man, and what you got was a backlash you didn't see coming. Well, I'm here to let you know it wasn't cool, it wasn't right, and if you ask me, it was on some bitch shit that doesn't fly in the streets.

Oakley told you he's not comfortable with five dudes getting in his face at once. Why would he be? You rush him like that, and his first thought is to swing. You're lucky all he did was finger push the dude in the temple. And you saw how strong that finger was, too. That finger is no joke. He finger templed the dude, and the dude looked like his head might snap off. Dolan, you really thought it was a good idea to send your security goon squad and surround Oakley like that? Come on, my man. That was uncalled-for shit, and the crowd and the people let you know what they thought. The streets and the media were talking, and they weren't feeling you, my man. And I was happy to talk to anyone who was on the fence.

The next day I had a conversation with Fox Sports' "all everything" personality Colin Cowherd. He didn't understand why Oakley meant so much to Knicks fans, which was so bugged out to me that I thought he was actually kidding. I told him Charles Oakley means the same thing to Knicks fans that Eric

Dickerson's offensive line meant to LA Rams fans. The same thing Rick Mahorn meant to the bad-boy Detroit Pistons fans. I had to explain this to him, which again was baffling, but I had no choice. Don Corleone is not Don Corleone if he doesn't have Luca Brasi. Oakley is our guy, and he don't sleep with no fishes.

He did it on the biggest stage under the brightest lights for ten years straight. It doesn't matter that those Knick teams didn't win a championship. Yeah, they came up short and it sucks, but we went down fighting, punching, finger wagging, and face smacking, and Oakley was on the front lines all day every day. And since we're on the subject of disrespecting classic Knicks players, I have to say there have been a few other notable shows of disrespect to classic Knicks players and family members in the James Dolan era.

James, you fired the great Marv Albert for questioning the team's choices and abilities? Motherfucking Marv Albert is as much of a Knick as Walt "Clyde" Frazier, Willis Reed, and Patrick Ewing. He was a damn ball boy for the Knicks when he was a teenager at the Old Garden on Forty-Ninth Street and Eighth Avenue. He got fired by Dolan for questioning the Knicks? What's the matter, man? I thought you had soul; I thought you understood loyalty. I thought you were in a blues band. What the hell, man? What's the name of this band you're in? Is it the Billionaire Blues Players of Madison Avenue? What are you even singing about, the sadness of chicken overcooked by a personal chef? The angry nanny who wouldn't do what you asked? Are you jamming to the pain of growing up wealthy and not understanding the common man? Send me the album; I'd love to hear it, as I'm a true lover of the blues.

We are New Yorkers, man. We stand by our team through thick and thin because it's in our blood, but you're making it really fucking difficult. Maybe you don't give a damn, since games are sold out no matter who's on the court or what the team plays like. I don't know, I don't work in the front office, but I'm damn sure getting fed up, and the Oakley incident only pushed us all closer to the edge. I don't need to recap the poor choices on and off the court by the Knicks' front office in the Dolan Era; it's too frustrating to articulate, I'll start to mumble. The fans, as frustrated as we are, keep coming back for more. We boo, we complain, and we yell on Tri-State area sports shows all week long, but it's falling on deaf ears. The Oakley incident represented all that frustration. Charles getting arrested inside Madison Square Garden after being accused of heckling owner James Dolan was Shakespearean, if you ask me. Oak said what was on every single one of our minds. He was the one who had the balls to say it, and he did. We all wanna go up to Dolan and say, "What the fuck have you done? You have taken the New York Knicks and turned us into a fucking joke since you got this building and team handed to you by your father, and you have ruined it, you fuck, you! Take your bullshit blues band and beat it, you spoiled little rich prick. And do yourself a favor and shave that funky-ass beard. You look ridiculous." All Knicks fans have thought about saying that to Dolan. I hear people practicing that exact speech in the streets before game time, but no one has the balls to say it. But Charles Oakley did. One of the toughest, most beloved players in New York City sports history said what we all were thinking, and he paid the price. The fucking irony. Charles "the Sacrificial Lamb" Oakley. He spoke for the people, and you locked him up. Get the fuck out of here with that behavior. Rumor has it that a Knicks fan went down to the police precinct and bailed Oak out later that night. Only in New York. Listen up. You don't want to turn the clock back to the Eighties when we could buy cheap seats and walk down and sit in the second row because the Garden was empty. You're pushing your luck. Never disrespect your top lieutenant.

The Eviction of Phil Jackson: An Absurd One-Act Play

NOTE: Sometime during the summer of 2017, there was a secret trial held in New York City in the U.S District Court of Appeals, where Phil Jackson and his team attempted to reconcile his situation with the New York Knickerbockers. These are the actual transcripts from this secret trial.

Inside the New York State Court of Appeals, the jury patiently assembles while Phil Jackson and his lawyer, Kurt Rambis, sit idly at the defense table awaiting opening statements from the prosecution. Michael Rapaport, representing himself, paces briskly back and forth in front of Phil and Kurt, staring them down as he prepares for the appeal. Kurt looks at him like he's crazy. Rapaport waves an index finger at Kurt Rambis and Phil Jackson as if to say, "No, not in here, you don't. This is my town."

Judge: Ladies and gentlemen of the jury, we will now hear the prosecution's argument in the case of Phil Jackson versus the City of New York. Mr. Jackson has been granted a hearing in the U.S. District Court of Appeals following his "release" from the New York Knicks organization. The court will now hear from the prosecution. Michael Rapaport will be representing himself in the case. Mr. Rapaport?

Rapaport stands up, takes out a cigarette, and puts it in his mouth.

Judge: Mr. Rapaport, there's no smoking in the courtroom.

Rapaport: Sorry, Your Honor, I didn't see the sign.

Judge: There is no sign. It's the law.

Rapaport: Are you sure?

Judge: Mr. Rapaport.

Rapaport tucks the cigarette back into his suit and paces in front of the jury, all of whom already look mildly concerned.

Judge: Mr. Rapaport, you have the floor.

Rapaport: Thank you, Your Honor. I was dying for that cigarette . . . I want you out of this city, Jackson.

Judge: This is no place for your personal sentiment.

Rapaport: It's all personal!

Judge: Either present your case or I'll toss it right out.

Rapaport: Sorry, Your Honor. Ladies and gentlemen of the jury and of this great city of New York, I ask you as both citizens and fans of the New York Knickerbockers to please understand that this hurts me as much as it hurts you, but there is no option here other than to keep Phil Jackson out of the great city of New York and away from the Knicks. Phil Jackson has been rightfully fired from the Knicks, and I'm here today to say we want him far away from the city. Let Phil Jackson go back to his happy place, where he can meditate, relax, and nibble on some peyote, or go to Peru, where Ayahuasca is all the rage.

Rambis: Objection!

Judge: Overruled.

Rapaport: I object to your haircut, Rambo! Did your head sleep with a raccoon?

Rambis: Excuse me?

Rapaport: What's the excuse?

Rambis: The hell does my hair have to do with anything?

Rapaport: Aha! That right there shows that everyone was out of touch in this Knick organization, including you and your goddamn barber!

Rambis: What?

Rapaport grabs a piece of licorice from his jacket and rips into it.

Judge: Mr. Rapaport, please refrain from eating in the courtroom.

Rapaport: I'm sorry, judge. My blood sugar's upside down, and no one told me not to eat in here.

Judge: There's a sign for that out front. Now move on.

Rapaport: Thank you, Your Honor, and I'm sorry, his hair's been an issue with me for years, and I did not mean to bring it up so soon in the trial.

Judge: Don't bring it up at all.

Rambis: Judge, can we move on here? My client is exhausted and has to catch a flight to the Bahamas, where he's going to get some R & R.

Phil smiles blankly off into the distance, then tries to catch what looks like a fly. But there is no fly.

Rapaport: Sorry to keep you awake, Phil; for someone looking to appeal a decision, you sure seem sleepy.

Judge: Mr. Rapaport, please continue.

Rapaport: Sorry, Your Honor; I just figured that if you want to make an appeal to come back to the city and maybe get your job back, you might want to be awake for the—

Judge: Mr. Rapaport!

Rapaport: We're all fucking tired, Your Honor!

Judge: Language!

Rapaport: I'm exhausted, too!

Judge: Moving on.

Rapaport: Phil, did you or did you not hire Derek Fisher to be the head coach of the New York Knicks?

Jackson: I did. He's so nice and little.

Rapaport: Did you consider that there were likely more qualified choices?

Jackson: Is your suit yellow?

Rapaport: What?

Jackson: I love yellow.

Rapaport: My suit is gray.

Jackson: Okay.

Judge: If we don't get on with this, I'll call for a mistrial. Continue, Mr. Rapaport.

Rapaport: Mr. Jackson, is it true that you once played against the likes of Wilt Chamberlain, Elgin Baylor, and Jerry West?

Jackson: Yes, that is true. We played against one another many times. I love the food trucks here. Am I coming back?

Rambis: Not yet.

Jackson: Okay. The gyros from the trucks in Columbus Circle are amazing.

Rapaport: You're gone, Phil.

Jackson: They're gone?

Rapaport: You're gone! You're whacked-out, man. Mr. Jackson, are you sure you even remember playing against those guys? Or is it possible that this is something you have forgotten completely and have no recollection of?

Rambis: Objection!

Rapaport: Snip the locks, four eyes, and stay out of the city.

Rambis: I haven't left!

Rapaport: You will soon.

Judge: Mr. Rapaport.

Rapaport: Look at your fucking dome piece, Rambis!

Judge: Mr. Rapaport! This is your last warning. Now move on!

Rapaport: Okay, not a problem at all, Your Honor. I'm simply asking if he remembers playing with such legends, because I can't figure out why the hell he hired Derek Fisher to coach the Knicks. Someone with absolutely no experience.

Rambis: Your Honor, this makes no sense, and I ask that it be struck from the record.

Rapaport: Not now, Mr. Mullet. I'm making all the sense!

Judge: Mr. Rapaport, please remain on point before I toss you out of here.

Rapaport: I'm sorry, Your Honor. This is all very emotional for me. I apologize. It won't happen again. Mr. Jackson, did you know that Derek Fisher had no coaching experience at the time you hired him, and that I, too, was available for the job?

Jackson: Why would I ever think about you as a coach?

Rapaport: That's a valid point but a stupid question. Aha!

Rapaport whips out two 8" x 10" photos of himself holding a giant trophy surrounded by a team of dirty-faced ten-year-old boys in shorts and football jerseys. He thrusts the photos in front of Jackson and Rambis.

Rapaport: I coached my son's flag football team full of snot-nosed, uncoordinated kids with no athleticism to the Los Angeles North Valley twelve-and-under championship.

Rambis: Objection!

Rapaport: That is true! You can't object to the truth! Stay in Peru!

Jackson: I've never been to Peru.

Rapaport: Lies!

Judge: Objection withheld, Mr. Rapaport. What does this have to do with Mr. Jackson choosing you as a coach? Stay on subject here.

Rapaport: Everything! It has everything to do with it! Derek Fisher did not have a coaching background. I did! Goddamn, it's hot in here. . . . It's sweltering. Can someone turn on the air-conditioning?

Judge: The air is on.

Rapaport: Oh, well, what's it on, Your Honor?

Judge: Seventy.

Rapaport: I like it at sixty-five, if we could make that happen.

The jury looks on in disbelief.

Judge: The air-conditioning is staying as is, Rapaport.

Rapaport: Not a problem, boss man . . . Mr. Jackson, are you aware that Derek Fisher was willing to fistfight his former teammate in the NBA, namely Matt Barnes, over a supposed love affair with a woman?

Jackson: I was not. How great is that New York skyline? And you know you can eat anytime of night here? I know a dumpling place in Chinatown that stays open until 3 a.m.

Rapaport: Are you on mushrooms, Phil?

Rambis: Objection!

Rapaport: Overruled!

Judge: You don't overrule. I do.

Rapaport: Are you on acid, Phil?

Judge: Mr. Rapaport!

Rapaport: I'm sorry, Your Honor, but you can't tell me Phil doesn't seem hopped up on something.

Judge: Continue. Please.

Rapaport: Ladies and gentlemen of the jury, need I remind you that Mark Jackson and a host of other more qualified candidates were also available for the Knicks coaching job at the time?

Jackson: I knew that.

Rapaport: Yet you chose Derek Fisher?

Jackson: I did.

Rapaport: This is absurd! He led us to the worst record in franchise history in 2015!

Jackson turns to Rambis and they have a quiet moment.

Jackson: Is that true, Kurt?

Rambis: It is, Phil. The team sucked.

Jackson: No one told me that.

Rambis: Okay, I'll look into why nobody told you about it.

Jackson: Thanks, Kurt. And could you look into those vape pens while you're at it? And see about investing in an ice cream truck, too.

Rambis: You got it, boss.

Jackson: Thanks.

Judge: Moving on. The courtroom will adjourn for lunch soon.

Rapaport: That's good, that's good. There's a great deli downstairs if you're into pastrami, Your Honor.

Judge: I'm not.

Rapaport: They make a wonderful knish as well.

Judge: I'm fine, thank you.

Rapaport: Your loss.

Judge: I'm sure.

Rapaport: Phil, were you aware that under your tenure, the New York players were getting robbed for their money and jewelry?

Jackson: I heard rumors.

Rapaport: Rumors? It's on record and in the news, as well as on video. Derek Williams had $750,000 worth of jewelry taken from his hotel room.

Phil turns to Kurt.

Jackson: Is that a lot?

Rambis: It is substantial, Phil.

Jackson: Shit. That won't happen again if they let me have my job back.

Rapaport: It ain't happening, hippie.

Jackson: He sounds so confident.

Rambis: And loud.

Jackson: We should all go to Rao's. What a sauce they make.

Rapaport: This is my point. The entire organization is lost. I'm talking about jewelry, and he's talking about meatballs.

Jackson: I don't wear jewelry. I like tie-dyes and loose pants. Feels great on my legs. Has a nice airy feeling.

Rapaport: You're gone, Phil. You're losing it. Cleanthony Early was robbed at gunpoint, and they even stole a tooth out of his mouth.

Jackson: That has to be painful. I have a great dentist. He has such soft hands.

Rapaport: Of course that's painful, but not as painful as having to admit you got your fucking tooth stolen! He's not Leon Spinks, for God's sakes!

Jackson: I don't understand.

Rapaport: Of course you don't understand. Maybe this will help. They robbed those players because the New York Knicks lost all respect in this city. You think the great Patrick Ewing would have gotten robbed for his gold molar?

Judge: Mr. Rapaport?

Rapaport: You think Bernard King would ever get jacked in his own town for the wisdom tooth right out of his mouth?

Judge: Enough!

Rapaport: Hustlers, pimps, and dope dealers cleared the way and protected the great Knicks like Willis Reed and Earl "the Pearl" Monroe. They wouldn't dare think about robbing them!

Judge: Please note that Mr. Rapaport has lost his way, and strike this information from the records.

Rapaport: I'll sell my own fucking tooth!

Jackson: Is this necessary? Kurt?

Rambis: Objection!

Rapaport: I'll take your fucking retainer!

Rambis: I don't have a retainer.

Rapaport: You should have one, Kurt. Your teeth look like shit. Let me ask you this, Phil: How about a curfew?

Jackson: God bless you.

Rapaport: I didn't sneeze! I said curfew.

Jackson: Oh.

Rapaport: People of the jury, I ask you to look at Mr. Phil Jackson here and realize that he is no longer fit to run this team, and that we must uphold the decision to keep him out of New York for the remainder of the Knicks' existence.

Judge: Mr. Rapaport, the jury will make their decision at the proper time. Please continue. And why are your shoes off? Please put your shoes back on.

Rapaport: Come on, judge, my feet are burning up.

Judge: Put your shoes back on!

Rapaport: Okey-dokey, you're the boss.

Rapaport unwillingly puts his shoes back on.

Rapaport: Mr. Jackson, did you or didn't you say you were going to have the Knicks run the famed triangle offense here in New York?

Rambis: Objection, Your Honor! That offense is not understood by many people, and we ask that you strike that statement from the records.

Judge: Motion denied. Allow for the triangle offense to be kept on record. Continue, Mr. Rapaport.

Rapaport: Of course you want it thrown out. No one understood the fucking offense! It didn't work here. It's like you were trying to teach trigonometry, Phil. No one gets the mystical "all for one, one for all, everyone has to touch the ball before shooting it" offense. It's over, Phil. This ain't Chicago, and Jordan ain't here. The triangle offense should be banished. Can we all wake the fuck up, please? You're gone, it's gone. Good-bye.

Judge: Watch your language in the courtroom!

Rapaport: How can you run an offense that you yourself have forgotten?

Jackson: It worked with the Bulls in '93.

Rapaport: That was twenty years ago!

Jackson: Has it been that long, Kurt?

Rambis: A little longer. Is my hair really that bad?

Jackson: I never noticed.

Rapaport: Phil, is it true or not true that you started directing tweets to your star player, Mr. Carmelo Anthony?

Jackson: Is he here?

Rapaport: Is he here? No, he's not here, and neither are you!

Jackson: Is he coming?

Rapaport: No.

Jackson: Good. We never got along.

Rapaport: No shit, you're not getting along. Mr. Jackson, you tweeted at him like you were a scorned teenage girl. You tweeted that he should leave New York and chase the championship elsewhere. Is this or is this not ridiculous behavior coming from the onetime head of operations of a well-known, legendary franchise?

Jackson: Is Porzingis on Twitter?

Rapaport: Judge, he's not even answering my questions.

Jackson: I love Porzingis. I'll tweet him. I'll miss him the most.

Rambis: Please don't.

Jackson: Okay.

Judge: Mr. Rambis, please advise your client to answer the question.

Rambis whispers into Phil's ear. Phil pops what looks like an edible.

Judge: Mr. Jackson, there's no eating in the courtroom.

Jackson: Sorry, judge. It's medicinal.

Judge: Excuse me?

Jackson: It's for my knees.

Judge: You're eating medical marijuana in my courtroom during your appeal?

Rambis whispers into Jackson's ear.

Jackson: No, sir. I'm not sure what that was. It was stuck in my pocket and my mouth was dry. It might be a caramel.

Judge: Mr. Rapaport, let's get moving here.

Rapaport: Judge and members of the jury, I am as upset as you are. I've shed many a man tear over this decision to pursue and uphold the eviction of the once great—and he was great—Phil Jackson from New York. This entire thing has given me a stomachache, and I already have an acid reflux issue and a number of gluten-related problems as well. It's kept me up for weeks on end, but I cannot waver on my decision to keep Phil from coming back here, and I ask you, the jury, to see it the same way. To quote former Knick legend Micheal "Sugar" Ray Richardson, "This ship be sinking." The New York Knickerbockers have never sunk so low, and the city itself has never been so uniformly together on one subject—that subject being the firm and permanent removal of Phil Jackson so we can return to being the greatest sports town of all time, a city that deserves a championship team, a team that can be proud to play in Madison Square Garden, the world's most famous arena! Phil, I want you out of the five boroughs before it's too late. And, Kurt, let's get real: you need to cut that ridiculous mullet that you call a hairdo!

Rambis: Objection!

Rapaport: Accept that you've got more scalp than hair, Rambis!

Judge: Mr. Rapaport, you're out of order!

Rapaport: No, Your Honor, *you're* out of order, *he's* out of order, *Phil Jackson's* out of order.

Judge: Mr. Rapaport, sit down!

Rapaport is in a leaning position, as if to touch his toes.

Rapaport: I can't, I can't, Your Honor. I got an issue here. I think my back locked up on me!

Judge: Mr. Rapaport, did you not hear me?

Rapaport is now back up and running in circles in front of the jury and the defense table, waving his hands in the air as if he's won the case.

Rapaport: We did it, we won, ladies and gentlemen of the jury! And, Judge, you can rejoice with me as well, because I know you want this burnout gone, and I know you want this appeal to fail and for him to retire and be done here! I'm well aware you canceled your season ticket package, Your Honor. Nobody wants to see it anymore. We the people of New York have removed Phil Jackson from this city once and for all!

Judge: Rapaport, you are in contempt! Sheriff, will you please remove Mr. Rapaport from the courtroom?

Rapaport: I'm a fucking winner. You're a loser, Phil! I took a group of ten-year-olds with no basic skills or proper diet plan to the flag football championship! What the hell have you done to my city? The Statue of Liberty is shitting her pants as we speak!

Judge: Mr. Rapaport, you're going to jail! I set your bail at five thousand!

Rapaport: That's good!

Judge: Now it's ten thousand!

Rapaport: Even better! At least it's less than what Phil paid for players who don't even want to be here! And I will happily do my time quietly, Your Honor. I hope they have TV where you're sending me. That way I might be able to see my dreams of living in a great sports town revived again!

The jury is going crazy, clapping for Rapaport. The sheriff cuffs him and takes him toward the exit.

Rapaport: My people, I have spoken! Grab me that cigarette from my inside pocket, will ya?

The sheriff finally whisks him out of the courtroom, the door closes, and the judge bangs the gavel.

Judge: Courtroom dismissed!

Phil Jackson lays his head on the table to take a nap. Rambis runs his fingers through what's left of his hair.

The courtroom goes dark.

Halftime!
My Spiritual Connection with the Housewives of Bravo TV

A while back I was sick of watching the New York Giants getting their asses kicked on *Sunday Night Football*, so I shut it off and went to see what my wife was watching in the bedroom. She was happily leaning into Bravo's *Real Housewives of Atlanta*. As I was coming down from nine hours of Sunday NFL football, I just put my head into the pillows and let the show roll over me. I had no idea of the long-lasting treat that I would be giving myself.

I couldn't believe what I was seeing. The women argued, laughed, and talked so much shit to each other that I had to take note. I asked my wife a few backstory questions about the relationships that were being slaughtered and reawoken within the same five-minute scene. I kept saying, "Yo, is this shit real? This shit can't be real." I couldn't believe there were real people behaving like this. I didn't believe these women were this funny, volatile, and open with each other, and it was all being filmed for TV. I was drawn in immediately. As soon as the episode ended, I wanted more.

I started binge-watching past seasons of the housewife shows like a pheen. I became a real-life Real Housewife junky. The shit was starting to cut into my work. I had things to do, lines to learn, and books to write, but I couldn't focus unless I was completely done with an episode. I couldn't fucking pause. As a prideful and seasoned shit-talker myself, I recognized the greatness of NeNe Leakes's ability right away. NeNe is a proud former stripper who has made the most of her time on these shows. After ten seasons on *RHOA*, she's carved out a nice career as an actress and TV personality. One of the things that helped her stand out was that she's a vicious and outrageous shit-talker who doesn't care about the ramifications of her tongue-lashings. She can also take it as good as she gives it, which is an underrated quality for a great talker of trash. I loved her instantly. NeNe Leakes in her prime on *The Real Housewives of Atlanta* was as entertaining and genuinely charismatic as Calista Flockhart was as Ally McBeal. I consider NeNe my vessel into the world of Real Housewives. She was so genuine and comfortable with herself, good, bad, and ugly (behaviorally speaking) that as an actor I found her inspiring.

Nobody exudes total relaxation in a Real Housewife as much as the great Bethenny Frankel. I refer to her as the Michael Jordan of Housewives because she left *RHONY* in her prime and did the unprecedented and came back better and stronger than ever. Bethenny is truly one of the best ball breakers I've ever seen on screen, or in real life, for that matter. She's a combination of a young Vince Vaughn and Seattle Supersonic Gary Payton when it comes to verbal warfare. She's funny, provocative, and self-deprecating. The fact that when she started on the *Real Housewives of New York* show as a regular girl who didn't know where she was going in life and eight years later created the multimillion-dollar Skinny Girl business is some true-blue, only-in-America-type shit. I have no idea how much money she's worth, but it's a fucking lot, and she did it all in front of the cameras. Getting to follow Bethenny through relationships, marriage, divorce, and having a kid all while listening to her talk some of the best shit you'll ever hear has been television entertainment at its finest. The whole idea of following sort-of-regular people on their personal journeys is always compelling. The Bravo Real Housewives series is truly documenting people's lives through thick and thin.

One of my favorite documentary films is the *Up* series, which has followed a group of British children from different backgrounds from the ages of seven through fifty-six, with a new documentary on the same kids produced every seven years, and it's still going. Film critic Roger Ebert considered it one of the great films of all time, as you see life change and evolve with all its unpredictability. I consider the Housewives shows a similar kind of documentary filmmaking, and the people on the shows are brave to let millions of people into their worlds.

Trust that I say this with the full understanding that if you have never seen any Bravo Housewives shows, these kinds of comparisons will make zero sense to you, and you might be saying, "What the fuck is Rapaport even talking about?" I get that, but you're the one who is missing out, my friend. Every Housewives table flip, wig snatch, or emotional tirade is your loss, not mine. You're missing out on some of the best entertainment of the last ten years. We're currently in the Golden Era of television, with so many great shows being created and so many different formats to watch. But don't forget that television was produced to bring simple entertainment into homes and to give families enjoyment. Yes, I love great, complex dramas like *Breaking Bad* and *House of Cards* just as much as the next person. And I also appreciate sitcoms like *Friends* or *The Big Bang Theory*. But I would put up the unpredictable family dysfunction of *The Real Housewives of New Jersey* against any Emmy Award–winning show. I will also put the wackiness of *RHONY* cast member Ramona Singer and the crying face of Beverly Hills newcomer Erika Jayne up against anything on Comedy Central. So, do yourself a favor the next time you've run out of games to watch or your favorite fancy-ass cold-case murder mystery show runs its course. Find yourself some Bravo Real Housewives and buckle your seat belt for good times and even some genuine, tear-jerking drama. Trust me: you won't be let down. Tell the Housewives I sent you.

Rapaport's Real Housewife Top Twenty Power Rankings, Volume 1

20. Dorinda Medley, *RHONY*: Immediate break-out star. The blue-eyed shit-talker has finger-pointing skills and hand gestures that commonly make traffic police stop and stare. Medley will mess things up but always "make it nice." Loyal to the core as she continues to stand by her longtime lover "Johnny Cleaners," who should be starring in his very own straight-to-video mob movies.

19. Shereé Whitfield, *RHOA*: Comeback Housewife of the Year in 2017. Has the best straight face in the game. Showed her vulnerable side in '17 but will still go toe-to-toe with anybody. Famously told NeNe Leakes to "fix her face" and became a viral sensation. Proudly built Château Shereé from the ground up, on her own dime.

18. Cynthia Bailey, *RHOA*: Beautiful fifty-year-old former supermodel will sometimes leave new viewers dazed and confused with her ever-changing wig/weave collection. Fashion maverick to some, style nightmare to others. Good natured and tries to avoid trouble, but proved she wasn't above kicking

a Bish when she got into a dust-up with a fellow Atlanta housewife.

17. Carole Radziwill, *RHONY*: Known to her friends as Radzy. Good natured but not innocent. Has been accused of being the most storyless housewife in franchise history. Recent concerns are mounting over her ever-growing collection of stray cats. Radzy made waves when she bagged a sexy twenty-six-year-old vegan chef named Adam, who could cook your pants off and bore you to sleep in the same evening.

16. Ramona Singer, *RHONY*: Gave the world Turtle Time, her signature announcement to her cast that she's about to get boozed up. Has more facial contortions than Meryl Streep could dream of. The zany and unpredictable stylings of Ms. Singer have left her castmates laughing, crying, and totally confused.

15. Kandi Burruss, *RHOA*: The good-natured Grammy-winning musician and sex-toy mogul doesn't start trouble but will not shy away from ending it. Burruss is a member of the R&B group Xscape. She's tough as nails and a reluctant but frequent on-camera crier. Kandi is a fan favorite who has often had to clean up her own mother's messiness.

14. Erika Girardi, *RHOBH*: Also known as Erika Jayne, the hyper-sexual, multi-award-winning pop singer. Girardi/Jayne was the hands-down Rookie of the Year in 2015. Her sharp tongue and "I don't give a fuck" attitude were an obvious threat to Beverly Hills' veterans. However, she lost her cool and some cachet in her second season with the now infamous "Panty

Gate" scandal and a disturbing crying face. Longtime wife of much older husband attorney, Tom Girardi, who bought her a Chagall painting for a million dollars.

13. Phaedra Parks, *RHOA*: The lawyer-mortician was the first Housewife to get fired publicly from the show. I predict she will someday return. This low-key shit starter and possible undiagnosed pathological liar has dealt with a lot during her tenure in Atlanta, and I wish her a speedy return to the Southern front lines.

12. Sonja Morgan, *RHONY*: Known to some as the Village Idiot. The sexy Upper East Side town house owner has a knack for hiring scrappy interns. Extremely open but classy about her past love life with Prince, playboys, and even Jack Nicholson. Holder of many secrets. Will talk herself into trouble and have no clue it's happening.

11. Luann de Lesseps, *RHONY*: This former countess has never shied away from her sexual escapades. Finally found "Tom" and got married despite the shitstorm the relationship caused in New York. A lover, not a fighter, the ever-controversial Lou has always done it her way.

10. Porsha Williams, *RHOA*: Has come a long way during her run in Atlanta. Married and divorced in front of our eyes. Started out as an innocent bootylicious Barbie doll and morphed into a wig-snatching machine. Porsha has evolved since she notoriously mistook the fugitive safe-house network known as the Underground Railroad for an actual railroad that simply ran underneath the ground.

9. Brandi Glanville, *RHOBH*: This quintessential shit starter is very responsible for taking the Housewives' drama to the next level. She came, she saw, and she trashed up the joint with reckless abandon. Although she's gone from Beverly Hills, she will never be forgotten. Her return would be a nightmare to some but also would be Bravo TV gold.

8. Lisa Rinna, *RHOBH*: The soap opera star and shampoo-selling icon brought the drama when she landed in Beverly Hills. Has shown that her acting chops are beyond what she's allowed to do on daytime television. Rinna can shed a single game-changing tear at the drop of a dime. Has stood in the pocket and stirred the pot with the best of them. I've heard Rinna is currently the patent holder and inventor of the Xanax smoothie. If that's right, and you ever have a headache or misalignment, she's your go-to gal for a quick fix.

7. Rosie Pierri, *RHONJ*: Not officially a Housewife and has no qualms about it. Rosie is a fan favorite on the Jersey show. Tough as nails, with a heart of gold. Pierri has tried to remain loyal to the whole crew despite the Garden State's propensity for chaos. Continually looking for love in all the wrong places. I hope this good woman finds herself a good woman to settle down with.

6. Kenya Moore, *RHOA*: Every show needs a great villain, and Moore plays it to the fullest. This former beauty queen could "twirl" her way onto Mother Teresa's bad side. She's the master of the hit-and-run. Loves to throw shade and act like it never happened. Has shown a softer side of late but will always be a natural "talk shit first, ask questions later" player of the game.

5. Teresa Giudice, *RHONJ*: Became a New Jersey icon with the "table flip heard 'round the world." Entertaining as Carmela Soprano. Spent one season in prison and kept her job. A "family first" type of broad with a gravity-defying hairline. We've watched her grow up before our eyes and bounce back from more adversity than arguably anyone in reality TV history.

4. Vicki Gunvalson, *RHOOC*: A true-blue Housewife Iron Woman. Often referred to as the Cal Ripken Jr. of reality TV because of her longevity and dedication to the craft. The twelve-year Orange County vet is the OG of the OC and will be the first to say it loud and proud. Salute legend.

3. Kim Zolciak-Biermann, *RHOA*: Some call her the Great White Hope of Housewives. Duked it out in the early years of Atlanta. Impact player as the show's only white girl. Her magical moments with her Sugar Daddy, the mysterious "Big Poppa," are not to be forgotten. One of the first to have her own spin-off series. This Southern baby-making machine is a shoo-in for the Housewife Hall of Fame. Married to NFL veteran Kroy Biermann.

2. NeNe Leakes, *RHOA*: The hands-down Queen of Shade. This magical wig-wearing housewife is a true Atlanta icon. Single-handedly brought the term "Bye, Girl, Bye" to the masses. A legend in her own mind and those of Housewives fans alike.

1. Bethenny Frankel, *RHONY*: Because duh! She built a life and a brand while being a ball-breaking machine. She will wind up as the silhouetted logo of the Housewives franchise like Jerry West is for the NBA.

23 Reasons Why LeBron Will Never Be Like Mike

I first heard about LeBron James the same way most of the world did: from seeing clips of him as a high schooler destroying poor kid teams like they were playing a different sport. It was impressive. Did he look like a bearded twenty-seven-year-old man? Yes. Was he dunking on freckle-faced kids from Ohio who looked fifteen years younger? Yes. But I was a believer. LeBron was the real deal and ready for the big time. He even answered media questions like a vet: "LeBron, as the greatest athlete in our city's history, do you feel you have to carry the torch, and does the pressure ever get to you?" LeBron came right back, prepared: "I've learned to tune out distractions and focus on the game at hand, so the answer would be no." What the fuck? Was Deepak Chopra his media coach? Who says that shit in high school?

Then he got drafted by the Cleveland Cavaliers, became Rookie of the Year, averaged over 20 points a game, and the stage was set. And I was all in! I really liked LeBron. I even met him early on in his career, and he seemed like a nice young man.

I bumped into him during his rookie year as I was leaving Jay-Z's 40/40 Club in Manhattan after a frustrating conversation with HOV himself about the importance and influence of

Brooklyn's own Dwayne "Pearl" Washington. HOV shockingly disagreed with everything I said, but we moved on. LeBron could not have been more polite after I literally bounced off his already cement-hard and giant nineteen-year-old frame. He said, "It's a pleasure to meet you, Mr. Rapaport. I'm a big fan, sir." And I always remembered that he called me sir, 'cause while it was nice, it also made me feel old. Part of me wondered if it was a backhanded compliment. Was LeBron secretly hating on me but covering it up in a nice-guy sandwich? Was he thanking me and hating at the same time? I am not sure he had all that on his mind, but after seeing him in the league over the past decade, I'm convinced he does have a secretly devious side—that at least sometimes the dude smiling for the camera is shitting on us when he gets home.

The first glimpse I saw of the real LeBron James was at the Celebrity All-Star Game a few years back. This was my territory. As many of you may or may not know, I was the MVP of the Celebrity All-Star Game in 2010. Look it up; it's true. For some reason, they kept me out of the game the following year, but it was probably a mistake. Rumors flew that some of the other celebrity participants couldn't handle my rants or hard fouls, but I'm sure that wasn't it.

Nonetheless, I wasn't in the game, but I had the chance to do some sideline reporting, and I was fine with giving other kids a shot at the MVP trophy.

I had my two sons with me, and after the game, we spotted LeBron. My kids are chill when it comes to the celebrity thing. It doesn't faze them. They've met a lot of people over the years, and they don't trip. But they wanted to meet LeBron and asked if we could go over and say hi. I told them of course we could. Now let me reiterate: My kids are NOT star-struck. For instance, we were once backstage at a Kanye show talking with Kobe Bryant,

Matt Barnes, and Kanye, and my youngest asked if we could go home so he could rest up for school! That's a fact, one you need to keep in mind here. They aren't easily impressed. So now the shit gets weird, and this is where King Jizzames fucked up.

I walked over to LeBron with my kids to say what's up. Everyone knows the All-Star Game is for the kids and about the socializing between players and fans. Well, the shit went south quicker than I expected. I said, "What's up?" to LeBron, and before I could even ask him for a picture, LeBron James iced me and my kids. He stuck his long-ass, tattooed arm out, didn't acknowledge me or even make eye contact with my sons. Instead, he turned his back on us and looked in the opposite direction like a scorned woman. Gave me the Heisman for real. My kids' faces dropped. And I was ready to fight the man-child. You ice me out, I don't give a fuck; you ice my boys out, and now we got a real fucking problem.

You've read about my past, LeBron; you understand the level of emotion I live with inside my body. I don't know exactly why LeBooBoo tried to play me out, but I did hear rumors later on that a situation arose in which a friend of a friend of mine knew a woman of a friend of his, and things got sticky between the friends. Regardless, it had nothing to do with me, and it definitely had nothing to do with my eight- and ten-year-old sons. And while I still want to fight him, I don't want my kids growing up without a father. I've been fortunate to be around NBA events for a long time, and I've met everybody, and LeBron is the only motherfucker to pull a fuck-boy move like that. It was blatant and it was personal.

LeBron, I know in your mind, somewhere in the back of that perfectly coifed, amazingly trimmed, bearded head of yours, you think you're the next MJ or that you've somehow surpassed Mike.

But you're not. And if you thought you were going to Be Like Mike, let me spell it out for you in a different way—you ain't. So I've compassionately and with much thought put together an exhaustive list of the twenty-three reasons why you will never be like Mike. Let us begin:

The Official Career-Spanning Twenty-Three Reasons Why LBJ Will Never, Ever Be Like Mike

1. **You shave your armpit hair.** The man we call King Fucking James shaves his armpit hair. This isn't a figment of my imagination. Homeboy shaves his pits. My sources tell me you also shave your chest hair. Who are you, David Hasselhoff? A six-foot-eight, 280-pound man shouldn't manscape. It's not manly. Let it grow. Let it dangle.

2. **You toyed with the numbers of legends.** You wore Michael Jordan's iconic number 23 when you came into the NBA in 2004; fair enough. You were on his jock, he was your idol, all good. Five seasons later, you suggested the league retire it. You even threatened to start a league-wide petition on some real *Mean Girls*–type of shit. Who made you jersey king? And to make matters worse, you were then wearing the number 6, which was Dr. J's and Bill Russell's number. So, it's okay for you to wear their numbers but not MJ's? You're better than the Doctor and the winningest player in NBA history, Mr. Bill Russell, now? What were you trying to say here? Now you're the one deciding who means more to the game? But the baseline SuckaShit you did was going back to wearing the number 23 in 2014. You're all fucked up and confused in the game, man. If you want to be like

Mike, pick your own number, stick with your own number, and create your own lane.

3. **Sneakers.** There's never been a better player with a worse shoe. I'm confused by this sneaker catastrophe. Is it made for basketball or hiking? The shoes take a half hour to get on and need to come with an instruction manual on how to lace 'em up. I'll say it again: great player, shit shoe. They should have named the shoe Irony by LeBron James. I can hear the advertisement in my head: "From one of the greatest players of all time comes a shoe you'll never, ever wear: Irony by LeBron James." Them shits look like overpriced combat boots. Matter of fact, give them to the troops; they're not for hoops. Maybe that should be the slogan: "For troops, not hoops." The shoe is an overpriced, overstylized disaster. Your latest 2017 joints have four Velcro straps and no shoelaces. Are they for playing basketball or checking into a psychiatric ward? You should've named these new ones Rubber Rooms. This ain't the Cuckoo's, and you ain't the Chief. Fix this fiasco.

4. **You gave yourself a nickname.** You don't give yourself a nickname, LeBron. Nicknames are given to you by writers, friends, teachers, or coaches. Let someone out there do it for you, LeBronBron. That's just some egomaniacal weirdo shit. Mike was given Air Jordan by other people, so was Magic, same with myself. You think I came up with the Gringo Mandingo on my own? No, I earned it.

5. **The Decision.** The Decision was a bad decision, LeBron. It was a travesty top to bottom. It was seventy-five minutes long and overproduced. What was the point of making it such a

production? To let us know you were leaving Cleveland? It wasn't the State of the Union Address. You're a basketball player leaving one team for another, not an actual king. You don't actually knight people and shit. But we all tuned in like idiots. You didn't even make the announcement until thirty minutes into the show. Finally, after boring us to tears, you announced you were taking your talents to South Beach. You then showed up in Miami for your personal pep rally, fireworks and all, declared you were planning to win not six, not seven, and not eight championships and made a spectacle of yourself. Cleveland Cavaliers owner Dan Gilbert was so pissed off by the way you handled the situation that he wrote a full letter in Comic Sans font. Then he slashed the price of your Fathead Poster to $17.41 because 1741 was the year Benedict Arnold was born. You made a circus out of something that should have been handled professionally. Very un-Jordan-like.

6. ***Sports Illustrated,* bully ball.** You had a right to sit out the 2016 Olympics, I can't even argue with that; rest your nerves. But my guy at *SI* subscriptions tells me you bullied your way onto the cover because everybody was talking about Kevin Durant going to the Warriors and not about LeBron winning his third ring. Look up LeBron's *SI* cover, August 8, 2016. It looks like a bootleg cover for a low-end fitness magazine. That's because my sources told me LeBully shoved his way onto that cover, and they didn't have time to do a presentable photo shoot. Kids dream about being in the Olympics their entire lives. And just when they get their shot to appear on the cover, you snatched the dream because you needed a

little Summer Loving? What kind of greedy shit is that? I'd bet my ass that some Olympic gymnast was scheduled for that cover. But Baby Bron Bron needed a cover story, so he ripped the hopes and *Sports Illustrated* cover dreams away from some five-foot-two female gymnast? Bad Bron Bron, Bad Bad Bron!

7. **The Big 3.** You created this monster called the Big 3. This is all you, trooper. No other star has ever left a team during his *prime* to go play with two other superstars during their *primes* to create a Big 3. This is all your doing. Every other team in the league is now forced to play catch-up because of this AAU friends and family bullshit you started. And don't try to compare the Celtics of 2008 to the Miami Heat. Kevin Garnett and Ray Allen were heading to their thirteenth year in the league when they arrived in Beantown—still very good but admittedly past their primes. The Houston Rockets' Barkley, Drexler, and Olajuwon crew of 1996 should've been called the Ghosts of the Big 3. That was literally a big fat joke that fell flat on its back and tore its Achilles. The Golden State Warriors drafted their homegrown Big 3 of Curry, Klay, and Draymond, and don't be mad at your former summertime workout buddy Kevin Durant for following your playbook and creating a Big 4. I'm glad he went to Golden State, and I'm glad they beat your asses in five games. That's what they call "a gentlemen's sweep." When you retire, one of the first things that will always come up is the fact that you left the league out of balance with your Big 3 Bullshit because you couldn't get things done the natural way.

8. **LeBron played water bottle tricks at the Garden.** On December 7, 2016, while a professional basketball game was taking place between the Knicks and the Cavaliers, you started flipping water bottles on the Madison Square Garden court like a ten-year-old hopped up on Cherry Coke and Now & Laters. My man, you don't ever flip water bottles in the Garden. You were doing the water-bottle challenge on the same floor Rocky Marciano fought Joe Louis. The same floor Ali fought Frazier. The same floor where Hulk Hogan dethroned the Iron Sheik! What the fuck is wrong with you, soldier? Mind your manners. You're lucky it wasn't in the days of Xavier McDaniel and the Late Great Anthony Mason. Xavier would have had you swaddled up real tight in a blanket and had you sipping out of a water bottle in his lap. The Garden ain't a playground, and we don't play children's games—unless, of course, Disney on Ice comes to town.

9. **Sitting out games.** People are traveling to come see you play, not to watch you cheer in sweatpants from the bench. That's like going to Disneyland and Goofy takes the day off. You wanna be like Mike or you wanna be like Goofy? The choice is yours. You know what that does to a child's head? Kids are like "Daddy, where's LeBron? I thought he was playing," and now the dad's a mess because he has to explain to little Harold why his favorite player is sitting out but joking around with the guys on the bench and leaping up and down with seemingly healthy knees. Plus, they're spending real money to see you. And you don't even stop to think about the family problems you're causing. Dad has to get home, the kid's crying, the wife's trying to calm the kid down, and Dad's stressed out wondering how a ball game

cost him $350 and he didn't even eat a hot dog. LeBron, you just caused a divorce. Think about little Harold and his sad father the next time you decide to sit out a game and rest. And don't try to blame it on your coach, Ty Lue; everyone knows that little fucker isn't calling the shots on that team.

10. **Mani-pedis.** Yo, my man, what's up with you biting your nails all the time? You nervous? What are you so nervous about? When you're on the bench, you're there to rest and absorb the game; it ain't a beauty bar. It ain't a nail salon in downtown Akron. You're giving yourself full manicures with fingernail clippers and nail files on an NBA bench. By the way, do you prefer glitter or classic French tips? I'm asking for a friend.

11. **Headband confusion.** Kids everywhere were throwing their headbands to the ground in confusion. LeBand, call your stylist and let's make a decision already. We can't rest not knowing what it's going to be. Kids are sitting in front of the TV waiting on the headband or no headband so they can get their wardrobe together. Pick a style, any style. You don't see Slash going from top hat to baseball cap and confusing the skinny-jeans youth of Rock 'n' Roll America. Settle on something. L.L. Cool J didn't take his hat off until 2013, and that was just to prove he didn't have ringworm.

12. **The flops.** "I love it when they call me Big Flopper." Shout-out to the great Biggie Smalls. I never read any Shakespeare talking about "Then the King flopped down for no fucking apparent reason and, yes, by golly, he did it again." Real kings don't flop, King James. You have an actual flop compilation

mixtape, for crying out loud. You don't believe me, look it up on YouTube. Type in "LeBron James flailing all over the fucking place" and see what comes up. Michael Jordan ain't got no flop compilation mixtape. Neither does Kobe. Not even Anderson Varejão has one. It makes no sense. You tell the press you're like a football player, but then you fall to the ground like Nancy Kerrigan when she got the baton from Tonya Harding. What's up, puppet legs? Are you made of Lincoln Logs? And the floundering arms on the way down are just embarrassing. These are the little details that keep you from true, unarguable greatness. Stop the flopping before the second mixtape comes out. By the way, the Draymond Green Ghost Flop of the 2016 NBA Finals should've gotten you a Flop Oscar. Even Bobby De Niro was impressed with that performance.

13. **Never entered the dunk contest.** Jordan lived for the dunk contest. He won some, he lost some, but at the end of the day he was all about them. He didn't become a superhero until he leapt from the free-throw line and threw it down. The world hasn't been the same since. You do 360-degree dunks on the layup line. You beast-dunk in games and the crowd goes nuts, yet you've refused to be in the dunk contest your entire career? One of the classic contests in sports doesn't get to see "the Chosen One" throw it down? It's upsetting. It's disappointing. It's selfish. Do you hate the fans, LeBooty? I know you've got crazy dunks up your sleeve. Let's see "the Thunder Shave"! Leap over two friends, finally shave every hair off your head, and throw it down. Get wacky with it. Even Dominique couldn't pull that dunk off. The fans want to see it. I want to see it. Your barber wants to see it.

14. **LeBron unfollowed the Cavs during the 2016 season.** You unfollowed your own team on Twitter? What the fuck is that? They call that Uncoupling, and Gwyneth Paltrow invented it. Whatever happened to a good ole-fashioned pep talk? What about a phone call to some of the players to try to motivate them? "Hey, man, we need to buckle down on D and get our shit together, and now is the time!" Instead you unfollow them? Then a Cavaliers reporter asked why you unfollowed your team on Twitter, and you got so offended that you walked off on some Marcia Brady girl-pouting shit. Men lead, they don't unfollow.

15. **LeBron blames.** On February 6, 2017, you openly cried to the press about needing a "playmaker." You actually told the press that your 2016 World Champion Cleveland Cavaliers, an already stacked organization, didn't have enough good players. Did Tom Brady ask for a third arm after winning the Super Bowl? Did Derek Jeter ask for a fourth supermodel when the Yanks won the World Series? Fuck, no! This was your yearly shit fit, the same shit fit you've been throwing since you went back to Cleveland. It baffles me and my people. Stop complaining to the press every spring and look in the mirror. Be the one to make the change, like the King of Pop said. You're the greatest playmaker in the world, so man up! Real playmakers do real things!

16. **What the hell is with the dancing?** You're playing patty cake with your teammates, turning the sidelines into an embarrassing episode of *Dancing with the Stars*. I see your teammates' faces, and they're not thrilled to be involved with this either. They'll never tell you, but as a person who reads

between the lines for a living, the team is praying the dancing stops. Trust me, the guys are going home to their wives like, "We don't know what the hell is wrong with him. I think I spun when I was supposed to finger snap, and LeBron went crazy. I can't keep up with the new choreography." Save the dancing for when you're home with the family or in the back of a club where no one else can see what the fuck is going on. The shit is corny, and you're making your teammates uncomfortable. Not to mention you're doing it in the faces of opponents while you're winning, yet you're not shaking guys' hands when you're losing. You ain't Danny Zuko, and this ain't *Grease*.

17. **Trying to get into the next *Space Jam* movie.** You're rumored to be attached to the *Space Jam* sequel? How the fuck are you going to be like Mike when you can't even come up with your own movie franchise? Let Bugs Bunny rest. He's tired. You want your own franchise? Bring the Care Bears to life. That's more your style. I'll make a call if you need me to.

18. **The Blood of David.** You got Israeli coach David Blatt fired in the darkness of the night like an episode of *Homeland*. What a *shanda*. (That means "shame," for all my non-Yiddish-speaking readers.) You publicly disrespected him, you pushed him out of the huddles during time-outs, and you wiped plays off his clipboard on national TV. I saw it all. You walked right by him and left his fist bump hanging. I understand if you don't get along and you don't agree on basketball philosophy or you don't see eye-to-eye—okay, fine, it happens. But you got David Blatt fired before the

2016 All-Star break, while the Cavs had the best record in the Eastern Conference, and you act surprised? You acted like you had no participation in it. This was some *Godfather II* LeCorleone James–type shit. Don't tell me you weren't the button pusher on this one. You wanted him whacked from day one, and you went to the mattresses to make it happen. The Cavaliers didn't get the most dominant player in the NBA's approval for this? GTFOH, man. You singlehandedly turned the country of Israel against you and all things Cleveland when you spilled the Blood of David and left the scene of the crime in the darkness of night. You handled the Blatt situation like a *pakhdn*. That's Yiddish for "coward."

19. **Rivalry shaming.** For some reason, you deny rivalries in your life. Rivalries are good, LeFear. They define you. Ali versus Frazier, Leno versus Letterman, and Fonzi versus the Malachi Brothers. These are real rivalries. You win some, you lose some, but don't deny they exist. You deny these rivalries because you think the competition is beneath you. Is that true, LeBron? You're so great that you're rivalry-less?

    Your Heat beat the Spurs in the Finals of 2012. The Spurs came back and knocked the snot out of you guys in 2013, and instead of seeking revenge for your embarrassing loss and giving the fans the tipping-point series and a great rivalry, you ran back to Cleveland with your tail between your legs. Four years later, after losing one championship to the Warriors and then coming back to beat them, you publicly say, "The Cavaliers don't have any rivalries." Even Riley Curry looked at you sideways, Bronny. You don't like Curry, he doesn't like you; the Cavs don't like the Warriors, and vice versa. That's called a rivalry. Go watch *The Outsiders*. The Greasers and the Socs hated each other, and we loved watching it. Stay gold, Ponyboy!

20. **Superteam Amnesia:** Immediately after the Warriors flushed the Cavs back to Cleveland in the 2017 Finals, you denied ever being part of a Superteam. Are you kidding me? You said, "I don't think I've ever been on a Superteam." Oh, you don't think you've ever been on a Superteam? You invented the Superteam, my friend. You made that statement in front of the entire world, and we were baffled. This was the most outlandish shit you'd said to date. The Miami Heatles set this Superteam bullshit off, and you were the orchestrator. The Kyrie, Kevin Love, Tristan crew you're a part of right now is a Superteam, and they've got the paychecks to prove it! You guys should play in capes, you're so super. Maybe you were disoriented because you got out-Superteamed by another Superteam, and that must be confusing. It's like building Frankenstein and then he tries to kill you. Don't be shocked. You created the contrived Superteam. Live with it. We have to.

21. **The elephant in the room.** You've never gotten hurt, LeBron, and that's a good thing; thank goodness for that. Throughout your magnificent career you have somehow, some way avoided a serious injury or even a strained anything. Even Mike missed stretches of games due to injury. Barry Bonds, Roger Clemens, and Lance Armstrong all suffered injuries as well, and, shit, they were on . . . let's just say vitamins. But you've avoided injuries altogether. Now, I know you take

great care of yourself. I read about it, I saw pictures of you at the juice machine, and I even tried to follow you on that special 2014 super summer cleanse. Pictures surfaced of a super-skinny you with half the muscle tone, and the streets were talking. You looked pretty damn skinny. Now, I'm not exactly sure, because I don't fact check and I don't have a staff to do it for me, but that was the same summer the NBA changed its drug-testing policy, wasn't it? Like I said, I don't know, and I'm not pointing fingers. I'm sure this is all just a coincidence.

When the 2014 season started, it was your first season back in Cleveland, and you weren't looking too LeBronish. You were nowhere near as physically explosive. No big dunks around the rim, and no power flops. You looked a bit slower, too. Hmmm. Then out of nowhere you took two weeks off to "rest." Personally, I was shocked, because you're such a fierce competitor, but I guess everyone needs a little rest. No injury reason was given; they just said "rest." During this "rest" period you went *back* to Miami, A-Roid's—I mean, A-Rod's favorite town. Then lo and behold, two weeks later you return to Cleveland looking strong as shit, weight gained and muscles toned. Man, I wish I could "rest" for two weeks and get cock diesel. Can you share with the world that amazing Miami Resting Diet? Anyway, I think it's great that you've never gotten injured, especially in a world where even Mark McGwire got hurt while he was on—*hachuu*! Excuse me.

22. **You lost in the Finals.** You've lost in the Finals so many times that it's hard to keep track. Mike never lost in the Finals. He

was 6–0. He never even needed a Game 7 to close out an NBA Finals. I'm a firm believer in the String Theory, LeBron. We are all interconnected. Hear me out. I see a sign. You're three and five in the Finals, Kevin Durant's jersey number is thirty-five, and Miami-based rapper Pitbull is known as Mr. 305. Do you see a connection? I do.

23. **Stop chasing ghosts.** The reason why you'll never be like Mike is because from the bottom of my heart I believe *you're better than Mike.* Not as a player—don't get ahead of yourself, Bron Bron. That ship has sailed. You're better than Mike as a star, as an example of what you should stand for as a celebrity in the sports world. You've spoken out on so many important issues throughout your career that Mike never even touched on. Social issues of race and politics you took head-on and made your voice heard. Your speech at the 2016 ESPYs was fantastic, bold, and brave. The public Donald Trump disses have been legendary and important. I couldn't stand your Miami Heat teams, but the Trayvon Martin acknowledgments were ballsy and were needed from such a cross-cultural superstar. RESPECT for all of it. Sincerely. I'm well aware of the millions of dollars you have personally donated to send kids to college, and now you're financing an entire school in Cleveland for at-risk kids. Nothing but pure respect and admiration for all that. I know you do a lot of good that we never hear about. It's awesome and inspiring, and maybe it should have been moved up in the chapter, but that's not what I do. The biggest mistake Michael Jordan made during his playing days was never speaking out on real issues. You've used your superstardom to kick ass for a lot of people. You've

inspired the next generation of star athletes to do the same. Stars get afraid to speak out and make a stand. You have done the opposite. Salute! So stop trying to be like Mike, my man, and just be yourself, LeBron. But the next time you see me with my kids, you better recognize.

Richard Williams's open proclamation of his daughters' takeover, Key Biscayne, Florida, 1999.
Al Bello/Getty Images

Venus and Serena Kicked All the Ass, but Richard Williams Is the Real MVP

Richard Williams, who is Venus and Serena's father, is the real MVP. The girls did the work, the girls kicked all the ass, but Richard is the MVP. Forget the fact that both of his daughters became two of the greatest tennis players in history, forget the fact that they came from a city where tennis was nonexistent, and let's also put aside the fact that he beat every odd stacked up against him to make it happen. We're talking about tennis, the whitest of the white, most country-club, blond-haired, blue-eyed, matching-plaid-shirt-and-shorts, stuffy, stick-up-your-ass sport ever—next to skeet shooting, of course. The man had vision beyond this world.

This is a guy who saw everything before it happened. Richard Williams wrote a seventy-eight-page life plan with a pen and paper, mapping out Venus's and Serena's entire futures, and it all came true. All of it. When his friends asked him if he thought he had the next Michael Jordan, he told them, "No, I've got the next two Michael Jordans." And he did! And he took no shortcuts. This wasn't a guy who had "friends" and connections in the tennis world. He didn't even want connections. He said fuck it and moved the family to Compton to raise them in a town that would reflect the harsh realities of life. He wanted Serena and Venus to see life's rough edges. Williams was a mad genius, plain and simple. He literally worked a miracle. He barely knew the game and was mostly self-taught. He learned tennis from videos, books, and a guy named Old Whiskey. True story. This man has something special, and we need to hear more about him. Richard Williams put the girls in a tight-uppity-ass tennis academy when they were four years old, but didn't like the way they were being coached, so he decided to take them out and teach them himself.

Richard Williams knew exactly what he was getting his daughters into, and he took it on, headfirst, and prepared them to do the same exact thing. He knew the scrutiny that black girls would get in professional tennis. It wasn't an accident that when Venus and Serena arrived on the pro circuit, their hair was beaded up and braided. That was a statement, and I fucking loved it. The statement was loud and proud that we are here and we want you to know we're here. We are Young, Gifted, and Black, and we're here to kick fucking ass. We're not going to act like we're just happy to be here. We're coming to fuck shit up. We're not going to answer your dumb-ass questions the way you want us to after we just lost a match, and if our opponents don't move out of the way when we're walking across the court, they will get bumped into with no apology.

The Williams sisters are game changers on so many levels, and Richard orchestrated the whole thing. The girls' worldwide coming-out party in New York City at the 2001 US Open was unforgettable. It will historically stand with Jesse Owens's, Jackie Robinson's, and John Carlos's accomplishments. Two black girls who are also sisters playing for a championship? It was magical. And Richard was brash, bold, and predicted the whole thing from day one. He ruffled feathers and scared the shit out of white people, and the girls backed it all up. By the way, I know their mother, Oracene, had just as much to do with the Williamses' success, but Richard was the one talking all the shit on the front lines, so he gets the chapter, but a strong shout-out to Oracene.

I don't get why athletes, coaches, and scientists are not desperate to track Richard Williams down and scan his brain to see what the hell is going on in there. The man is a total original. The Williams sisters are the best to ever do it, they did it their way, and they created an entire genre that should be called Smash-Mouth Tennis. Professional tennis will not be the same when they finally retire from years and years of Ass Kicking and Complete Domination.

The odds of anybody coming out of Compton and making it in pro sports are astronomical. But the odds of two black girls coming out of Compton and making it in pro tennis don't even exist. The best thing about it was that Richard Williams didn't give a shit about any odds. He made his own odds. He had the vision and the grit, and he never let the people forget where they came from. After Serena won her first Grand Slam in '99, he grabbed his nuts and yelled to the crowd, "Straight outta Compton, motherfucker!" Then he went and got nineteen-year-old Serena a $12 million deal with Puma. Thank you, Richard Williams, for being a crazy-ass Compton sorcerer and for bringing the world your two amazingly gifted and completely classy kids. And thank you for never giving a fuck what people thought about it. You're really the MVP.

Phife was easily the biggest sports fan I ever met.

Phife Dawg: Words from the Five-Foot Assassin

When Malik Taylor, better known as Phife Dawg, passed away on March 22, 2016, the world lost a great artist and a great man. His family lost a son, a brother, and a husband, and a lot of us lost a valued friend. And A Tribe Called Quest fans lost one of the most beloved and influential performers in modern American music. What may surprise some is that the sports world also lost the biggest fan I ever met.

In 2011, I had the pleasure of directing a documentary on my favorite group, A Tribe Called Quest, and got to spend a lot of time with Phife. Any big fan of the group could tell he was a sports fan by the way he dressed, in baseball hats with matching jerseys, and by the many sports references he made famous in Tribe songs:

"Scenario": "Hey'yo Bo knows this, and Bo knows that, but Bo don't know Jack, 'cause Bo can't rap, so what do you know, the Di-Dawg is first up to bat."

"8 Million Stories": "With all these trials and tribulations, Yo, I've been affected, and to top it off, Starks got ejected."

"Steve Biko (Stir It Up)": "Hip-hop scholar since being knee-high to a duck, the height of Muggsy Bogues, complexion of a hockey puck."

Those were just a few of the lyrics Phife kicked with sports at the heart of them. On Tribe's final album, released in October 2016, hearing Phife rhyme "John Wall" with "Chris Paul" and then saying "Boy, I tell you that's vision, like Tony Romo when he's hitting Whitten" was chilling to hear, but it's exactly what any Tribe fan would expect.

I knew he loved sports, but I had no idea how passionate he was about them until I started to talk to him during the filming of the movie. He was truly a fanatic. He loved pro football, college football, baseball, pro basketball, and college basketball. He knew the history of the leagues and the players in all of them, and would argue, rant, and debate anyone at any time about whatever topic they wanted under the sports umbrella. The last few years before he passed, Phife started making the rounds on many sports podcasts and TV shows. He was like a kid in a candy store when he was live at the desk on ESPN with Scott Van Pelt. You could tell he was having a ball. I know this was a path he was going to take had life not cut him short.

The first interview I shot with him was in his house in his Carolina Room. He had a man cave/sports room painted in North Carolina's baby blue. He had UNC memorabilia and photos all over the wall and loved to talk about his favorite Carolina players, their teams, the wins, and the greatest losses. Listen to me: I love talking sports any day, anytime, but Phife was on another level. I swear, he was always looking for a way to segue a conversation into sports, and when he did, that train didn't stop. He would reference moments and periods of his life based on his sports memory, and, believe me, it was vast and it went deep. If I asked him about the *Low End Theory* record from 1991, he would say,

"I remember that tour, because we were in Milwaukee, and I saw Brett Favre give it to the Vikings while I was in a hotel room before the show." Every interview would start with a musical subject, and he would take it right to the sports world. I could be asking about a song or a lyric or a time in the group's career, and somehow we'd end up talking about why he couldn't stand Duke. I would agree with him most of the time, too. I told him, "I couldn't stand fucking Christian Laettner either, but I'm trying to make a Tribe film here, Phife Diggity. Can we talk Tribe?" He would laugh and admit, "I know, I know; I just love sports so much, man. What was your question?" So, finally I realized I couldn't show Phife without having him talk about his love of sports and athletes. I told him, "Let's just get it all off your chest, and I'll film you talking about everything you feel about sports."

A chunk of that material wound up in the film, but still 80 percent of it couldn't make it in, since it was a film about the group. So, in his honor, here are a few words verbatim from the one and only.

Phife Dawg, aka the Funky Diabetic, During Our Filming of *Beats, Rhymes & Life: The Travels of A Tribe Called Quest*

Michael: Okay, let's do your favorite little men in NBA history.

Phife: Okay, this is a tough one, 'cause me being a little dude myself, I have a bunch of dudes I really like, but my five favorite little men in NBA history are . . . this is a good one . . . Kenny Anderson, Mark Jackson—I'm biased to New York, obviously, because we are the home of the point guards, or better yet, the point gods. So, Kenny Anderson, Mark Jackson, Kenny "the Jet" Smith, and then I got to say Allen Iverson, Chris Paul. Can I tell you what athlete I compare myself to as an MC?

Michael: Yeah, who?

Phife: I would compare myself to the Boogie Down Bronx's Rod Strickland. He was an ill point guard, he had flavor, everybody respected him, plus he was a pass-first point guard but could get his points whenever he wanted and whenever the team needed it. I also compare myself to him because a lot of times people will overlook him when they talk about dope guards of his era.

Michael: All right: Five favorite big dudes?

Phife: Kareem Abdul-Jabbar, Shaquille O'Neal, Moses Malone, Hakeem Olajuwon, and . . . I'm having a hard time with one more . . . Patrick Ewing.

Michael: Damn, it took that long for you to give Pat some love, Phife? You been on the West Coast too long?

Phife: Yeah, I'm bugging. Sorry, Mr. Ewing.

Michael: Let me have your five running backs.

Phife: My five favorite running backs: Barry Sanders, one, Tony Dorsett, two, Walter Payton, three, Eric Dickerson, four, and I'm having a hard time with one more.

Michael: Earl Campbell?

Phife: Earl Campbell's a great one, but I'm going to pick one for right now—Marshall Faulk, matter of fact. Marshall Faulk. I had to put him in there. He's one of my favorites. Absolutely. You gotta give me ten, Mike! Let me get ten, son? No, I'm just playing.

Michael: Yankees or Mets, Phife Dawg?

Phife: I'm from Queens, so I'm supposed to bleed Mets, but they piss me off every year, so I rock with the Yankees pretty much. Y'all see the hat. There's no other team in baseball history that should ever wear pinstripes. The Phillies should get rid of the pinstripes, because when I think of the Phillies,

I think of Mike Schmidt when they won the World Series in 1980 with the burgundy *P* and the powder-blue jerseys and stuff like that. They didn't have pin—oh yeah, they did have pinstripes on their home jerseys, the burgundy pinstripes, but they should get rid of them. Only the Yankees should wear pinstripes; the Mets shouldn't even have no goddamn pinstripes, you know what I'm saying? So, the Yankees are that team, straight up and down.

Michael: Hoya Paranoia and the Big East of the Eighties.

Phife: Oh, man, that has to be the greatest time in college basketball outside of Magic and Larry going at it in '79. The Big East was the greatest. You, of course, had the Beasts of the East, Pat Ewing at Georgetown, along with Reggie Williams, who went to Dunbar High School in Baltimore, Maryland. They had the squad; I'm just going to keep it at that. At Villanova you had Ed Pinckney and the McClain boys, nonrelated but they could both play. Dwayne McClain and Gary McLain. They were dope.

Michael: Saint John's.

Phife: Queens representation. I loved that squad. Saint John's, we had Mulley, you know what I'm saying? One of the baddest, slowest, but illest shooters in the history of the NBA. He's done it all, Olympics, everything, you know what I'm saying? The Redmen also had Willie Glass, Mark Jackson, and Walter Berry, Shelton Jones—they had the crew back then.

Michael: Syracuse had—

Phife: Syracuse had the great Dwayne "Pearl" Washington from out of Boys and Girls High School in Brooklyn; later on they had Sherman Douglas, they had Lawrence Moten, they had Adrian Autry from New York, and they also had

Derrick Coleman, Detroit's finest. High-jumping Steve Thompson. Jim Boeheim had a crew, Ronny Seikaly. Syracuse was the bomb back in the Big East. Who else was there? Pitt had Charles Smith and Jerome Lane. Remember when he shattered the glass? So, Big East basketball was top-notch. I used to keep my eye on the ACC, too, because I can't forget my Carolina Tar Heels and James Worthy. James Worthy is the reason why I became a fan of the Tar Heels and I still am till this day, you know what I'm saying? I can't talk about anything ACC basketball–related without talking about Lenny Bias, God bless him. He was really that dude representing University of Maryland. I was actually hyped that the Celtics drafted Lenny Bias. But Big East basketball was really it. I enjoyed growing up in the Tri-State area; that was the bomb. Oh, and then Providence, shout-out to my man Abdul Shamsid-Deen; Rick Pitino was coach, the coach of Florida, Billy Donovan, Billy the Kid, he was a point guard, and he was killing everyone the year Providence made it to the Final Four. I think that was 1987, right? He was getting busy.

Michael: Good shit, Phife!

Phife: I can keep on going if you want.

Michael: Ha-ha, I know, I know, but let's talk about the *Midnight Marauders* record now.

Phife: Bet!

If Iron Mike Tyson Can Find Inner Peace, So Can I

I love Mike Tyson. Straight up. I've been a fan since he was on the cover of *Sports Illustrated* when they called him Kid Dynamite. They talked about Mike knocking out twenty-five-year-old men when he was twelve. He was five-foot-eleven and 190 pounds with lightning speed in middle school. The article said every punch he threw was thrown with bad intentions, and they were right. Everything Mike was doing as a kid had bad intentions. He had it rough, no doubt. In and out of juvenile prisons his entire childhood, he couldn't see the light from the Brownsville streets where he was raised, or where he raised himself, I should say. Mike grew to be loved, hated, feared, and respected during his career. He lived the dark and the light like no fighter we've ever seen.

On top of the world one moment, then sent to prison in his prime. Number one fighter in the world, rich beyond his wildest dreams, then lost it all. Mike was a true product of Brownsville, Brooklyn. I personally thought I knew Mike's full story until I saw his one-man show on Broadway. The show not only blew me away but also clarified a connection I had felt with Mike Tyson all these years.

Mike was raw, honest, and ripped wide open on that stage

telling his life story. He was present and didn't hold shit back. I was blown away. He was so relaxed, he even shouted me out during the middle of the show like a seasoned comic living in the moment. He was midway through his story about going to prison, looked right at me, and said, "Oh shit, Michael Rapaport. I know you know about this shit, Rapaport." What the fuck? He was talking to me during the middle of his sold-out performance. I didn't know what to say. I was stunned. I didn't know Mike Tyson even knew who I was, and now he was shouting me out in front of two hundred people. I was also thinking, What the hell do I know about prison, hookers, or beautiful pageant girls? But then I thought about it for a minute and realized Mike was just relating. He was saying Rapaport, you know about pain, you know about life's ups and downs, you know what the fuck is real. I was back in.

I didn't come from where Mike came from, I didn't live his life, I didn't win and lose millions, but that wasn't it. I was a flawed human being who made a shit ton of mistakes in relationships, in marriage, and with my kids, just like Mike did. I wanted second chances the same way Mike did. That night, Iron Mike got my respect on a whole new level. I could feel him up there. His anger, his erratic behavior, his inability to articulate when emotionally heated, I felt all that. Mike was all of us, and he articulated that beautifully. Iron Mike Tyson was doing a one-man show, and I was having an emotional experience watching it. It blew my mind.

Mike talked about wanting to be a good father and how he fell short. That shit gut-punched me. I know how that feels at times. I haven't always made great dad decisions. Mike was up there talking about losing his cool. I've lost my cool more than a few times. I've got that Mike Tyson ready-to-blow shit in me all the time. Similar fucked-up thoughts are in my head. I'd love to punch someone in the face, I just don't have a place to do it; and for the record, I don't like getting punched back. I heavily related to Tyson's difficulty articulating his feelings and emotions.

Mike Tyson has said some wild shit during his time in front of the camera. I remember a spectator once yelled to Mike during a prefight press conference, "Put him in a straitjacket," and Mike told the guy he was going to fuck him until he made the guy fall in love with him. Mike lost it, and I fully understood. Mike had that mental-warrior shit going on. I got the same thing in a nice-Jewish-boy kind of way. The way I used to go into my auditions when I first started acting was 100 percent inspired by Mike Tyson. I swear to God, I walked into auditions like Mike Tyson walked into the ring. I was nuts. I was definitely trying to make up for the fact that I was probably under-skilled, but it worked.

When I went in to audition for the movie *Zebrahead*, I looked through Adrien Brody and said, "No, motherfucker, this is my shit right here. Sorry, my man, take your skinny ass home and work on your piano playing, because this one is for me. Don't even fucking think about it." He looked at me like I was nuts. I took that Tyson shit, ran with it, and got my first part. I did the same damn thing with *Beautiful Girls*. You think every other actor my age wasn't up for that part? Every one of them was in there. I was prowling the hallway like Mike Tyson then, with no socks and a ripped towel for a shirt. I told these motherfuckers, "Go home, get the fuck out of my way, this is me, this is my day and my movie—plus I think I have a man crush on Matt Dillon and need to be around him for as long as possible."

Did Mike's attitude get in his way occasionally? Sure, it did. Did he scare off a few journalists when he told them they had to leave or very bad things were going to happen to them? Yes. Have I said things to people in my life that I shouldn't have? Have I snapped on a motherfucker who asks some stupid question that I didn't feel like answering because I was in a bad mood? Of course I have. But that was the shit I needed to work on. That's what I was relating to most in Mike's story—trying to be a better human being. Mike's honesty was what I most respected. He was unapologetic and honest to a fault at times.

Mike spoke to Matt Lauer in an interview and told him, "If I'm drinking, I think about suicide." Tyson was talking about having suicidal thoughts like I talk about wanting an egg salad sandwich.

They brought Mike to a sober living conference, and the first thing out of his mouth was, "I've been lying to everyone here about being sober. I'm a vicious alcoholic, and I haven't stopped drinking." They brought him in to talk about the benefits of being sober, and he told them he was drunk. Honesty—flawed motherfucking honesty! I wish I could be that raw. I want to be that raw. I want to admit to my demons way more than I do.

Mike told Lauer in that same interview, "I hate myself. I'm trying to kill myself every day." Here's the former Heavyweight Champion of the World saying he wants to kill himself every day. Mike put a finger to his temple and said, "It's hard to live up here. No one's seen what I've seen. None of these fighters, none of these athletes; I'm the king of the barbarians. I'm a monster."

Mike Tyson: You're not a monster; you're a flawed motherfucker like the rest of us. Yo, Mike, thank you for that brave and ballsy one-man show and for letting me know that if the former baddest man on the planet can start humbling himself and trying to find inner peace, a loudmouth punk like me can start trying, too.

Great in the Ring, Shitty in Life

Floyd Mayweather is amazing in boxing and a prick in life. And I mean that from the bottom of my heart. Floyd, you're a jackass. I don't care that your footwork is second to none and that you made Canelo Álvarez look like an amateur when you fought him. I don't care that you took Manny Pacquiao apart like he was thinking about being president of the Philippines for the entire fight. It doesn't bother me that your counterpunching might be the best in the game and that no one can touch you with your peekaboo style. I get it. You mastered boxing, Floyd. But you act like a clown. You throw money in the air at strip clubs and you hit women. Kids everywhere are watching you saying, "If I make Floyd's money, I can buy a Bentley, throw money on a thick, fat-ass stripper, and beat up a girl!"

Wake the fuck up, Floyd! It's not too late. I know you don't want to be a role model. But you are. Yeah, man, that's the way the world works. You play a sport, you become the best, you make millions, and people look up to you. I don't make the rules, Assweather.

So, stop riding around your house on a Segway, chasing 50 Cent around like a girl trying to get an autograph, and get your life straight.

I want to talk to you one-on-one. Just me and you. We get in a room, we sit down like gentlemen, and we get into that fucked-up head of yours. Give me ten minutes. I know life wasn't easy for you growing up. The abuse, the poor upbringing, a family full of fighters—I get it. Life isn't fair, Floyd, but we can talk it out. The problem is I just know how that conversation would go:

Me: Yo, man, thanks for sitting down with me.

You: You see my Instagram where I took a shit on a pile of money?

Me: No, I didn't see that.

You: Shit on two million in cash.

Me: What's with the woman-beating? Floyd, where did all that come from? I mean, I know you said you came from a tough background, but come on, man.

You: This watch is worth half a million. I push a button and shit calls a helicopter.

Me: Yo, you're avoiding everything.

You: What do you want to know?

Me: How one of the greatest fighters to ever get in the ring can be so fucked up in life.

You: Yo, I bought two hundred pairs of red Yeezys.

Me: Fuck this.

I don't like you, Floyd, and I really wanna like you. I was sitting on the edge of my seat watching you and Manny go toe-to-toe, and I was praying Manny was going to take your head off. I was yelling, "Come on, Manny, where's that footwork, those angles, and those heavy hands? Come on, Manny, kill the body and the head will fall! Manny, what the hell, man, you can't be that into running for political office!" And I got nothing.

Then I had to go back and rewatch your first fight with Marcos Maidana because I just knew I was seeing a guy coming at you like a tank and landing blows. So, I went back and watched the fight, and you know what, Floyd, you little bling-bling, beat-a-girl, fake, drinking, club-lovin' degenerate gambler hoe? He didn't land one blow on you! This motherfucker had the entire world thinking there was a way to beat Floyd Mayweather, and the guy didn't touch you. You leaned back with that half flat-footed defense, hiding in your clavicle, and you moved a centimeter left and a centimeter right, and Maidana didn't do a thing. You got my head all fucked up. But I still had hope that someone was gonna get you.

So here comes Canelo Álvarez. He's going to come in and show you what the youth of America looks like. You want to play with Instagram, Floyd? Here's a kid who grew up on this shit. He knows Snapchat, too, and he's coming in like a redheaded fire engine ready to put out your bitch-made fire!

And then you did it again. I'm yelling, "Come on, Canelo, do something! You're twice his size, you're eight years younger, plus you're a redhead!" Everyone knows redheads got that anger shit in their DNA. I never met a calm redhead. Even the redheaded women I know are angry. It's something in the orange. I don't know; I'm not a scientist, Floyd. Here comes Canelo looking like a ripped version of Malachi from *Children of the Corn* (who, by the way, I was in acting class with in '89). Every scene Courtney Gains did was about torture. I wanted Canelo to whoop your ass. Then the opening bell rang, and Canelo second-guessed his entire career.

This was supposed to be the "Super Kid"? This was the kid who was going to prove to the world that Floyd Mayweather was beatable? You stood back, pawed the jab, snapped it when you had to, and then smiled and landed a left hook to the ribs as if it was a punchline to a joke. Fuck you, Floyd. Canelo telegraphed the right hand so badly that you got a haircut before it landed. Kiss my ass, Floyd. Fuck you for being so great in the ring and so shitty in life. Just sit with me for a minute. I can help:

Me: Floyd, you think you would have walked through guys like Marvin Hagler?

You: You ever seen sunglasses with diamond-encrusted rims?

Me: If you fought Tommy Hearns, who was six-three, one hundred forty-seven pounds with that reach and the best right hand in the game, you think you'd win?

You: You see that new iPhone eleven? Shit makes you a pizza just by asking. I got two hundred of 'em.

Me: Fuck it.

Floyd, I know I'm not going to get a chance to talk to you, but I am going to give you some unwarranted, unwanted, unheeded advice: Clean up your life game, Floyd. Clean it up. No reason to throw money in the air on social media when motherfuckers are out there starving. No reason to post pictures of your gold Bentley when kids looking up to you might never have the means to get that car—not to mention seven out of ten people who drive that shit are assholes. You flaunt shit in people's faces so badly that your own people robbed you and you ended up catching a case for kidnapping! Your own people, Floyd!

You did sixty out of ninety days for domestic abuse, and this wasn't your first offense. Floyd, get into therapy, man. I don't care if you take a note from Russell Wilson's "I quit pussy" playbook. Give yourself a time-out, Floyd. There's still time. Make it happen. I'm here for you. Get at me!

The Great White Hype of Ronda Rousey

Now, let it be known that I don't hate Ronda Rousey. I like Ronda Rousey. I love what she did, and I respect the hell out of the hard work she put into her sport. She's a high-level, well-trained, first-rate, disciplined athlete. She won a bronze at the 2008 summer Olympics in Beijing, and that shit is very real. However, you people at Business Insider fucked up when you gave her the title "The Most Dominant Athlete Alive." I don't know Business Insider, and they seem like some clickbait bullshit, but what business are they actually inside of? Not the sports business. You put Ronda Rousey ahead of Serena Williams, LeBron James, Tom Brady, Usain Bolt, and a gang of other athletes who are still dominating to this day; where the hell was your head? To me, this is a black eye for journalism. "The Most Dominant Athlete Alive"? She wouldn't be the most dominant athlete in my neighborhood. Maceeba Jonas was. I saw Maceeba beat up two burnouts during lunchtime and walk back to class like nothing had happened while smoking the cigarettes she jacked from them. She was dominant regardless of her age advantage due to her being held back twice. Ronda was knocked out by Holly Holm weeks after the article came out. The Most Dominate Athlete Alive was punched in the face and was not looking very dominant. It was upsetting, but not an upset.

Again, Ronda's personal story is great: it's heartwarming, it's authentic, and it's a true rags-to-riches story. She was homeless at one time in her life and truly became an iconic athlete in the new millennium. Inspiring narrative, absolutely. You know what else is a great story? The Life and Times of Amanda Nunes, an openly gay Brazilian chick who came from the bottom of the bottom of the *favelas* in Bahia, Brazil, to dismantle Rousey in forty-eight seconds. That, my friends at the Business Insider, is real domination. Has Nunes appeared on any magazine covers since? Is she hobnobbing with Ellen DeGeneres? Is she swimming in endorsement money? Fuck no: she's back in the gym trying to stay out of the Brazilian ghettos.

Now, this isn't Ronda's fault; this is the media's bullshit buildup—the same shit they do in boxing when they get a decent-looking fighter with okay talent and they want to build a star. We know the game. The entire media buildup of Ronda Rousey was some classic "Great White and Hope" shit. They took it too far and way too fast, and Rousey was the one who paid the price. The beatings she took were, in my opinion, avoidable if they would have given her some time to train as opposed to worrying about getting her to the photo shoot so she could help blow up your sport. Do me a favor and save terms like "Most Dominant Athlete Alive" for people like Steph Curry, Michael Phelps, or even that ball kicker Lionel Messi. People who dominated for long periods of time. You cannot be the most dominant anything at 11–0, and that was her record at the time the article came out. I was 19–0 in seventh-grade slap boxing matches, and no one said shit about me! Did I have a nine-inch reach advantage because of a growth spurt no one saw coming? Yes, but I wasn't being heralded as the most of anything! I'm begging you guys to stop giving titles like this away. I get it, I know, you're building a product. But don't do it at the expense of cheapening your sport, endangering your athlete, and tricking the public.

Side note: I wouldn't last ten seconds in the ring with Ronda. I'm flat-footed and don't do well in tight spots. Anyone puts me in a headlock, I fake my own sleep. I don't blame Dana White either. He doesn't write the pieces in these magazines. His job is to sell tickets, and he's doing what he has to do. I like Dana. Sure, we don't hang out much, but I do have his cell number. Plus, he's gotten me tickets, and I hope he doesn't stop. Get at me, Dana.

Why Boxers Make More Money Than MMA Fighters

I enjoy watching UFC and I want to see the sport grow, but I do think they need to figure out a couple of things. The way it's going, there will never be a UFC fighter making Floyd Mayweather money (unless they are fighting Floyd Mayweather ala Conor McGregor). You know why? Because there are too many ways to lose in the MMA and shutter your career while it's on the rise. In MMA, you may be the best wrestler in the game, and then you get knocked out by a boxer and the train stops. You may have the best stand-up game in the UFC, but you didn't prepare for the ankle lock. You may be a jujitsu master but didn't see the judo coming. Fighters need momentum to build careers and make big money, and in the UFC, it's too tough to build real momentum. Boxers generally have been doing one thing for much longer.

Boxers usually start when they're about seven years old. You fight in the amateurs and tournaments every week, and you build your amateur record running around the country with your family in a van. If you show any promise, you go international and fight around the world. If you shine there, then you may fight in the Olympics, and by that time you've got about sixty or seventy amateur fights under your belt and you're only seventeen years old. Now when you get out of the Olympics, people know you. The world's been watching you, and the promoters are circling. You've been building a fan base, and millions of people have heard your name. Now Bob Arum or Dan Goossen or Don King or Lou DiBella signs you to build your pro career. But they will not rush you like the UFC did Ronda Rousey. Mike Tyson was 22–0 before you ever saw his face on the cover of *Sports Illustrated*. Ronda was 11–0 and already starring in movies and landing on magazine covers.

The media also needs to stop portraying boxers and MMA fighters as equals in the ring. It's ridiculous. Would a grappler, who is trained in submissions and knows how to choke you out with your own shirt, beat up a boxer in the street if he got him on the ground? Of course he would! *But*, would a well-trained boxer dismantle any MMA fighter with limited boxing experience in a boxing match? Yes! You know who never, ever makes these comparisons? Boxers and MMA fighters, because they know more than anybody that they are two different sports. Why the fuck are they even having these talks on TV and radio sports shows every single day? It's like wondering if Michael Phelps would best Usain Bolt in NASCAR. They're both the fastest in their sports; how would one hundred laps at Indy turn out? Who gives a flying fuck? Shut this conversation down once and for all.

And I'm begging you, please, don't let Mayweather fight McGregor.

If Conor McGregor fights Floyd Mayweather, I may never order another boxing match in my life. I will not pay my own hard-earned money for that bullshit circus-act fight. And, Floyd, if you take that fight, shame on you for embarrassing the sport that made you rich and famous. McGregor is a loudmouth tough guy who, oddly enough, stole his entire persona from Money Mayweather, who stole it from Ali, who took his animated style from pro wrestler Gorgeous George. Conor is great at MMA, but let's not get it twisted. He's not going to stand a chance at beating Floyd, Canelo, Triple G, Terence Crawford, Manny Pacquiao, or any other top-twenty-ranked boxer. So, I hope by the time this soon-to-be-bestselling book hits the shelves, that fight will have never happened. You saw what Floyd did to Manny, and you saw what he did to Canelo. If that's not enough to let you know what he would do to basically an amateur boxer in Conor, then I don't know what to tell you. Again, I respect the shit out of MMA and the UFC, I'm a fan, but chill the fuck out. Once again, Conor is on that great-white-hype train like Ronda was. If you fight Floyd, you could get hurt. You might get hit so hard in the liver that your leprechaun tattoo could fall off. No idea if you have one, but that shit could happen. You've been warned.

Rocky *Is Great, but Not the Greatest*

There's an ongoing debate regarding what the best sports film of all time is. It's a favorite topic for many people, it's a sports blogger's dream to discuss, and it's something anyone who loves sports and film has sat up and argued about for years. Usually the lists look something like this:

10. *Field of Dreams*
9. *Miracle*
8. *Slap Shot*
7. *The Bad News Bears*
6. *All the Right Moves*
5. *Caddyshack*
4. *Friday Night Lights*
3. *White Men Can't Jump*
2. *Hoosiers*
1. *Rocky*

This is a damn good list of films, and most of these make my top ten, too. Every one of these films strikes a different chord. I want gritty, I go with *Hoosiers*; if it's a Sensitive Sunday, I'll throw in

Field of Dreams; or I could just watch *Caddyshack* or *Slap Shot* and enjoy a good laugh. And, of course, *Miracle* is always good for some inspiration.

Of course, any list of mine will always have *Rocky* near the top. *Rocky* was a life-changing movie experience for me. I saw it twenty times in the theaters when it came out in 1976. My sister took me the first time, then I saw it three times with my mom, five with my dad, and eleven anyone else I could tag along with. I can tell you anything and everything about that movie. It's probably my favorite movie of all time. Just thinking about *Rocky* gets me up and out of the house.

I also stand by *Rocky II* as being a totally underappreciated, high-quality film, with one of the most spine-chilling moments in film history. When Adrian wakes up out of her coma and tells Rocky she just wants him to do something for her, and Rocky says, "What's that?" and she tells him, "Win, win," and then Mickey says, "What are we waiting for?" it rocked my fucking world, and may be the best moment of any *Rocky* film ever. I'm having a hard time not doing push-ups for no reason right this very second.

Rocky III had its magical moments, too. You know you can't go wrong with Mr. T's Clubber Lang. And don't even get me started on Burgess Meredith as Mickey. I'll put him up there with the greatest characters ever to grace the screen in any genre of film. Even in *Rocky V* he had his one and only flashback scene where he says, "Get up, you son of a bitch, 'cause Mickey loves you." That moment was as inspirational as any TED Talk could ever dream to be. That's the beauty of the great sports films. They inspire!

When I watch *Rudy*, I still get emotional and cry against my will because it's so damn uplifting.

My Rocky *love is as real today as it was in 1976.*

Karate Kid is a dope sports film, and I'm not even sure if karate is a sport, but I'll be damned if I'm not waxing on and off for hours after watching that great piece. *Major League* with the pre–Tiger's Blood, "Winning" Charlie Sheen is amazing and still has a crazy cult following to this day.

The list goes on and on, and if you wanted to, you could break them down into individual sports. *North Dallas Forty*, *Any Given Sunday*, and the original *The Longest Yard* go down in football. *Miracle* and *Slap Shot* take hockey; *Field of Dreams* and *The Natural* might take baseball, and, fuck it, let's give *Happy Gilmore* and *Tin Cup* golf. Denzel Washington gets his own sports subcategory: *Hurricane*, *Remember the Titans*, and *He Got Game*: all great flicks, and Denzel never disappoints; I don't care if you give him a basketball or an airplane while drinking, he's a true acting beast!

Ali gets his own documentary section. *When We Were Kings*, *Soul Power*, *A.k.a. Cassius Clay*, *Muhammad & Larry*, and *The Thrilla in Manila* are all next-level documentaries.

ESPN's 30 for 30 series has made dozens of incredible top-ten-worthy films: *Winning Time: Reggie Miller vs the New York Knicks*, *The Fab Five*, *Catching Hell*, *The Announcement*, and *Survive and Advance* are all worth watching as soon as possible. I didn't even mention the sheer brilliance of *When the Garden Was Eden*, directed by maverick disruptive filmmaker Michael Rapaport. And the best of the entire bunch, *O.J.: Made in America*, won the 2016 Oscar for Best Documentary. The list is never-ending, my friends, but it's about to end, because not one of the films I just mentioned is the best. The best, my readership, is yet to come, and you're welcome!

The Bronx Bull, the Raging Bull

Raging Bull is the greatest sports movie ever made. Not only is it the best sports movie ever made, it's the best *film* ever made. Strong statement? I think not. This masterpiece transcends the sports genre and stands alone as a cinematic endeavor by the master himself, Martin Scorsese. I'm sorry, Mr. Balboa, I really am.

I don't need to give you the obligatory description of *Raging Bull.* If you haven't seen it, crease the page right here, put down this book, go watch it, and thank me later. This is not an inspirational tale, this is not a motivational tale. This is the in-depth story of one of the saddest, most complex characters of all time. The story is gut-wrenching, and what Martin Scorsese and Robert De Niro pull off is nothing short of miraculous. There are no shiny lights, uplifting speeches, comebacks, or heroic moments in *Raging Bull.* Jake LaMotta, played by De Niro, is an abusive, jealous, self-destructive motherfucker, and we love every single moment of it. All Jake's flaws, vulnerabilities, and pain make him relatable and bring him to life like no character in any film I can think of. It's not an easy film to watch, but it's not supposed to be. Life ain't easy to watch either, and no film mirrors life's depth of personal demons the way this masterpiece does. It's my number one, folks, and I'm sticking by it.

These are my fifteen rounds and reasons why *Raging Bull* isn't just the best sports movie ever made but the best film ever made.

Round 1: Bobby De Niro

What hasn't been said about Robert De Niro's performance in *Raging Bull*? It's a game-changing moment in acting. De Niro took everything that had ever been done on film before him and brought it to a new plateau, a level we haven't seen since.

It's a Big Bang moment in acting. You hear about method acting and living the part—well, De Niro reached the method acting mountaintop, and no one's knocked him off. It's hard to argue what's the best when it comes to art, because it's subjective, but this performance forced every actor and actress to rethink what was possible when it comes to character. De Niro looked and moved like a professional boxer, then gained sixty pounds to play out-of-shape LaMotta during his demise. The physical performance of Robert De Niro gave him the freedom to become LaMotta. Every blink, gesture, and breath Bobby D took as Jake LaMotta is a living organism and is as believable as anything we've ever seen on screen. He was in a zone you see only once in a lifetime. De Niro set the benchmark for what a person strives to achieve when taking on a role. Without De Niro's performance, we don't have Benicio del Toro, Christian Bale, or Leo's crowning moments in cinema. Next time you see Denzel, ask him what he thinks about *Raging Bull*. He'll probably sit down and have a moment with you.

Round 2: The Opening Credits

The sequence, which is shot in still frame over opera music, lets you know you're in for something huge. It's a painting. It's the

Sistine Chapel of opening sequences. De Niro dancing around the ring in slow motion sets the tone like no opening before it or since.

Round 3: Joe Pesci

This was Pesci's first part in a legitimate film. He was vivaciously alive, vulnerable, and real, and brought straight-faced humor and pain as Joey. Pesci went on to become one of the world's most beloved actors. He was nominated for best supporting actor but lost to Timothy Hutton in *Ordinary People*. The first time I ever got drunk in my life was on the set of *Beautiful Girls*, and I had to let Hutton know how I felt about him beating Pesci for the statue in 1980. That didn't go well at all.

Round 4: *Cheers*

Remember the guy who played Coach on *Cheers*? He was a journeyman actor named Nicholas Colasanto, whose biggest break before *Cheers* was playing Tommy Como, the mob boss who pushes LaMotta to throw a fight. He passed away during the third season of *Cheers* and was replaced by then-unknown actor Woody Harrelson. No *Raging Bull*, no Woody Harrelson, which means no *White Men Can't Jump*. You're welcome again!

Round 5: Cathy Moriarty

Her raspy voice alone should've gotten her an award. The first time she appears in the film, kicking her legs in the pool, stunning like a Fifties pinup girl, is one of the greatest introductions to any character in film history. This is arguably one of the sexiest sports film performances, along with those of Susan Sarandon in *Bull Durham*, Rosario Dawson in *He Got Game*, and Rosie Perez in *White Men Can't Jump*.

Round 6: Humor

Even though the *Bull* is emotionally dark, it's also funny as fuck. The humor comes from Pesci and De Niro's arguing over the most basic of life's things. They're like some sort of violent Laurel and Hardy. The "Hit Me in the Face" scene is like the Abbott and Costello "Who's on First" classic. Joey trying to tell Jake to get in shape for a fight by explaining, "If you win, you win; if you lose, you still win; just get down to 155 pounds, you fat bastard. You understand everything—do you understand that?" makes no sense and complete sense all at the same time. They pulled off the humor where it seemed impossible.

Round 7: John Turturro

One of the most underrated actors of the last twenty-five years. He auditioned over and over to be a part of *Raging Bull*, knowing it was going to be special. A young Turturro wound up having just a single line in the film but got to sit at the table with De Niro and Pesci during one of the scenes at the Copacabana. You can see him at the 22:15 mark of the movie.

Round 8: Cinematography

Every ounce of the black-and-white cinematography is perfection. Shot by Michael Chapman, the boxing scenes are so seamlessly put together that it's hard to make sense of when shots start and when they end. The boxing in the movie is a choreographed dance of beauty and violence. The fight scenes are shot like horror films. The brutality and violence are felt through the camera. One of the most memorable shots in film history is the "Blood on the Ropes" shot at 1:41:26 that single-handedly articulates everything that is violent about the sweet science.

You can watch the movie with no sound and still witness pure art in cinematography.

Round 9: *Boogie Nights*

Paul Thomas Anderson, the director of *Boogie Nights*, borrowed so many moments and ideas from *Raging Bull* and Scorsese to make his classic porn tale that he could have named it *Boogie Bull*. From the close-ups of the old-fashioned camera flashes to the long, steady camera shots to the most obvious final scene of *Boogie Nights* when Dirk, played by Mark Wahlberg, sits in front of the mirror, goes over his lines, and then whips out his prosthetic piece. This scene is lifted almost shot-for-shot from *Raging Bull*'s final scene.

Round 10: Life Lessons

"You never got me down, Ray; I never went down." There are so many life lessons in this film that inspire me to this day. Jake tells his wife after losing a controversial fifteen-round decision, "The people knew, they knew! They knew who the boss was. The judges didn't know. Who knows what happened with them—the people knew!" I find this dialogue so inspiring. This is something I say to myself when I'm feeling underappreciated, misunderstood, or taken for granted. I say to myself, "The people know what you're about, Mike, the people get you. Producers, agents, nerds, and judgmental hipster fucks wanna pass judgment, they don't wanna give you a shot, they don't wanna figure you out—fuck 'em. The people get you, the people know, they know." Try it. Next time you're feeling like you're not being heard or appreciated, ask yourself if the people know what you're all about, and if the answer is yes, trust me: you'll start to feel a little better about yourself. Fuck the judges. The credit goes to those in the ring. There are so many *Raging Bull* pick-me-up lines that I'm surprised they haven't released a book of haikus from the psyche of Jake LaMotta.

Round 11: "You Fuck My Wife"

A shocking yet classic line that goes down in the annals of history of cinema's greatest dialogue. "If you build it, they will come" is meaningful, the janitor's speech to Rudy will pull you out of the dark, but Jake asking Joey if he fucked his wife is a moment you can never forget. It's so disturbing that my sister pinched me on the arm in 1980 when we saw it for the first time in a movie theater on Second Avenue. The danger and dysfunction of that scene is beyond any sports film moment.

Round 12: Editing

This was the start of an incredible partnership between Martin Scorsese and film editor Thelma Schoonmaker. She has cut and pieced together every Scorsese film since. They're the Joe Montana and Jerry Rice of filmmaking.

Round 13: "Get Your Shine Box"

You know Frank Vincent even if you don't know his name. He's the shiny, gray-haired, raspy-voiced actor from almost every mafia TV show and movie of the last thirty years. He's the guy who tells Joe Pesci to "Go get your fucking shine box" in *Goodfellas*. Frank made his film debut in *Raging Bull* and is so real that you think he's just being himself.

Round 14: Marty Scorsese

I got to interview Martin Scorsese about *Raging Bull*. If you listen to the interview, I sound like I'm floating in outer space for the entire time because I couldn't believe it was happening. He told me this, a golden nugget I will never forget for as long as I live: "I took everything I knew and everything I had and put it into the film. I put everything on the line—my money, my health, everything. The film was everything I was looking for. For me, it was about finding my soul again." Martin Scorsese was cemented as a true artistic genius after *Raging Bull.* He went as deep as he could go to reclaim his soul, and you can see and feel it all up there on the screen.

Round 15: The Eighties

Raging Bull was nominated for six Academy Awards in 1980. It lost Best Picture to *Ordinary People*. But in perfect poetic justice, after ten years, all of the most respected film critics in the industry took a vote on best film of the Eighties, and *Raging Bull* won by a landslide, solidifying the masterpiece for what it was. No sports film has ever been voted best film of an entire decade. None. The people knew, they knew!

Caitlyn, Caitlyn, Caitlyn

Don't get me wrong, I've been a fan of Bruce Jenner's since the dude won the decathlon in the '76 Olympics. The shot put, javelin, sprinting, high jumping, winning it all with Marlboro Man chest hair; that shit makes you one of the greatest athletes of all time. I was only six, but I was ready to grow some chest hair after watching his run for gold. Bruce was on the cover of Wheaties and *Playgirl*, two covers that don't have shit to do with each other, but that's how insanely popular he was. He was one of the most famous people on the planet. Came from nothing and made something of himself. Dude was married, making nine grand a year while his first wife was supporting him, and he was training his ass off in his spare time. He was a man out of his time. After competing, he was writing books, racing cars, and making money. Bruce was a corporation. And then it happened. He got mixed up with the Kardashians and ended up on that show, and it all went fucking south. Didn't you get the memo, bro? You go into that house a man and you come out fucked up. I don't know what sort of voodoo pussy is happening over there, but no one is safe. Especially not a man. Check the records. It hasn't been pretty for any of them.

Lamar Odom goes in as a first-round draft pick NBA superstar with amazing potential and comes out hanging on for dear life after overdosing on crack cocaine, fuck pills, and white girls from a whorehouse in Nevada. That's an epic downfall of sad proportions. Then you got my little man Ray J, who starts out with a promising career, sleeps with Kim on camera, dives into that legendary apple, and never makes another good track again. The dude got that snapper, and where's his voice? Check the snapper. Is there a recording studio in her ass? I have no fucking clue, I'm just calling it like I see it. Then Kanye, one of the best beat makers and rappers in the game, goes in, and two years later he's crying onstage and referring to himself in the third person. What the fuck part of the movie *Get Out* didn't you get? And shit, I'm not even blaming them for everything.

I know you were confused, Cait; you said it many times: you felt like a girl growing up, you had female feelings. I get it; I'm confused every day of my life. It's the fucking way you're going about it all now that you're Caitlyn. I'm not a fan, and it has absolutely nothing to do with you being transgender. That might be my favorite thing about you. Someone wants to be what they feel deep inside and wants to transition, then guess what, I'm all for it. Come on out. Let's go. I'll hold your hand and throw on some heels for the fuck of it. I grew up in Manhattan, I saw it all, I didn't discriminate. I walked out of my place on the Upper East Side, said "What up?" to Genie, the giant transgender woman on the stoop, and went about my day. Shit did not bother me at all. Never has, never will. But there's just something I'm not feeling here about you, Caitlyn, and I think I know what it is. You should not be the face and the voice of the trans community. I don't think I'm alone in my thinking either. As a matter of fact, I know I'm not alone. Anyone who lives in Hollywood knows

Yum Yum Donuts is a great hang for the trans community, and when I'm getting my coffee-and-donut game on, we talk. And they ain't happy either.

These Hollywood streets are talking, Caitlyn. You think you represent what they've been dealing with for most of their lives? You've got $50 million in the bank from that fucked-up TV show, and now you're the self-anointed voice of the transgender people? You may have started with little, but you've led a privileged life for at least the last thirty years. Many of these people have been ostracized, beat up, left for dead in the streets, and addicted to drugs and all other types of bullshit, and you're wearing Manolo Blahnik shoes and $6,000 orange dresses, popping up on Diane Sawyer talking about voting for Trump. I don't think you represent them at all, girl. You're with Trump, and you think you're representing the LGBTQ community? You aren't clear how Trump and his crew feel about the LGBTQ community? You're on national TV talking about not regretting that you voted for him? Trump doesn't give a fuck about proven scientific facts; you really think he gives a fuck about you? We got a problem here, my friend.

Where the hell is your head? Oh, I know where it is—it's in the bank, where all your money is! You know if Trump could, he would lock you in the closet and never let you out. This is the guy you're voting for? The guy who said people can't use the bathroom they identify with, the guy who opposes nationwide same-sex marriage? This is your guy? Who are you fighting for, LGBTQ, the transgender community, or the rich white motherfuckers who make sure your money is safe? Because it can't be for everyone, my friend. Think it over, Caitlyn, before they turn on you. And let's be honest, you ain't that exciting to watch on TV to begin with. Yeah, I said it. Maybe you're just not that interesting.

If you're on the number one reality show in the world as a famous man and then you're transitioning into an even more famous woman and your own spinoff show gets canceled, guess what? You're fucking boring, Caitlyn. Once again, I'm not here to bash your choices, and I'm damn sure not here to bash your community, but I am here to let you know that it's offensive to the people in the struggle when you're popping up as the public face of the transgender world with $24,000 worth of gold on your neck and voting for that fuckface Trump, who can't stand you.

And on a side note: you claimed to have known that O. J. Simpson was guilty and you kept it to yourself. Yeah, I read the article. You told my man Andy Cohen that you and Robert Kardashian both knew that fucking guy was a murderer and you didn't say shit about it. Get with the program, homegirl. Come get some coffee and donuts with the me and the good folks at Yum Yum's sometime.

Stickmen: The Ultimate List of Great Stickmen, Part 1

I was lucky enough to work with Sylvester Stallone on the great ensemble film *Copland*. I knew when I got the part that I was going to fan out on Stallone, so I had to keep it all in check. *Rocky* is one of the reasons I first considered becoming an actor. I'm not joking. I saw the movie, I ran outside, I challenged every kid on the Upper East Side to a fight, and then I decided to become an actor. That movie changed my life for real. I don't trip out on a lot of people, but here was one of my idols in life. On the first day of shooting, I spotted him smoking alone off to the side, enjoying his peace and quiet. First off, the fact that he was smoking a cigarette threw me the fuck off. John Fucking Rambo doesn't smoke cigarettes, does he? Instead of leaving him in peace to enjoy his smoke break, I walked right up and told him how *Rocky* inspired me. He could tell I wasn't joking around and was cool as shit about it. I threw a few *Rocky* lines at him, and I'm telling you the god's honest truth: Sylvester Stallone was coming right back at me with the next line in the movie. I was tripping out. All of a sudden me and Sly are straight up doing scenes from all the *Rocky*s. I was Pauly, he was Apollo; I was Adrian, he was Rocky; I hit him with some Mickeys and he came back with Rocky. It was unreal.

It was a dream come true until the director came over and said, "Michael, you have to stop talking to Sly about Rocky, man; we're shooting *Copland* here." So, I had to quit distracting him. But before I left Sly alone, he dropped some shit on me that I'll never forget. I asked him about Burgess Meredith, the legend and actor who played Mickey in the *Rocky* films. Without missing a beat, he tells me, "Not only was Burgess an amazing actor, but he was a real stickman." A what? "Oh yeah, the man was great with the ladies. He was a notorious cocksman, one of the best of all time." I was stunned. Seriously? The little old guy from *Grumpy Old Men* was a world-class stickman? A cocksman?!

This is the actual day on the set of Copland *that Stallone declared Burgess Meredith the Consummate Stickman, and life was never the same.*

I had to recalibrate my whole thought process. I had heard about Warren Beatty in his day, and of course I heard about Elvis and the ladies, but Burgess? What was I going to hear next?

Abe Vigoda had his loaf out on the set of *The Godfather*? Stallone was dead-ass serious. Burgess Meredith was a World-Class Stickman. So, in honor of all the great stickmen out there, here is a completely-fact-checked-yet-absolutely-based-on-nothing, guaranteed-not-real list of the real stickmen.

Webster-Rapaport definition of a Stickman: A man with the innate, god-given ability to bed many, many women while having none of them speak poorly of him and continue on with his blessed wonderful life of sleeping around with no strings attached or regrettable repercussions.

Now, let me be clear: there's a big difference between a stickman and an irresponsible scumbag. Anyone can use fame to pull out the loaf, drop it on a stranger's shoulder, and roll the dice. That's not what I'm talking about. I'm NOT talking about Trump's "Grab 'em by the pussy" shitbag talk. That's scum-bum, bush-league bullshit. That's shit people say when the only way they get laid is by paying for it or "owning" a building that's not really yours but saying it is. I'm talking about a gentleman who does what he does and no one gets hurt. A man of honor, who, when it's all said and done, women don't bash or slam to their friends. I'm talking about a man who does his thing and gets street compliments and receives wonderful praise in certain circles. I'm talking about the All Stickmen League of America. And I'm only dealing with America because I don't feel like getting into Latin American bullfighters, European soccer players, and any of that Australian rugby shit. They can make their own list. This is ours. Good old American stickmen. Let's begin.

Prince and the Purple Loaf

Prince was a World-Class Tiny Purple Stickman. Rest in peace and test the Purple Piece. Prince was the eighth wonder of the world.

He was four-seven, wore high heels, was better looking than most women in makeup, could still do the splits when he was fifty, and ran shit like the mini-pimp of Minneapolis. Prince was pulling out the Velvet Loaf and laying down high-level game for years. He had white, black, Asian, all mixes, all races, all religions, all nondenominational orgy-type shit on lockdown. Prince's bedroom looked like an orphanage full of beautiful female adults and sometimes animals. Who the hell knows what was going on in there? Prince had a velvet rope in front of his bed! He had Apollonia and Vanity all in the same decade, same movie, and same city. You ever been to Minneapolis? Do you have any idea how tight your high-heel guitar game must be to lock down two 10s in a city that lives in snow? You have any idea how tight your game has to be to wear a long, flowing dress, black fishnet stockings, high heels, and a painted-on mustache and lay it down like that? Prince was crossing borders before the shit was okay to do. And he wasn't afraid of big women either. Prince showed up with Kirstie Alley at an awards show in the Eighties, and she was carrying him like a baby. He didn't give a fuck, and neither do I. He rolled into the Grammys with two models and a baby bottle around his neck. Prince recorded a stick session with Kim Basinger in her prime, and her moans made it onto the *Batman* soundtrack. Are you hearing what I'm saying here? He put her moans on one of the biggest-grossing film soundtracks of all time. Yeah. Basinger's getting the Raspberry Beret peter-piper-picked-a-pepper-pussy treatment, and she was so happy with my man that she let him put it on the record. Did she have a hard time getting another acting job later? I don't know. I don't discuss careers here. The point is, Prince had it all on lock, and he's first ballot. Prince had a "Don't talk, just walk next to me and look straight ahead and nod" rule with women. So, RIP to Prince and the Purple Loaf.

He's one of the greats, and I'm proud to acknowledge him here at the top of the list.

Derek Jeter

He's sometimes referred to as Your Favorite Stickman's Favorite Stickman. I gotta talk about my man Derek Jeter 'cause he kept his shit low, but we knew what was happening. Yeah, Derek, we read it in the papers, we saw it in the *Post*, we knew you had shit poppin', but you never talked about it in public, and that's a true prerequisite for a gifted stickman. And you did it in the greatest sports market in the world. This wasn't some small-town smash-and-grab shit. This was New York City, where everyone knows everything, and they follow you around all day every day, and no one knew where the fuck you were, and then you just pop up on a street corner with a five-foot-eleven brunette fresh off the boat from Brazil sent to America to model her feet, and no one hated you for it. We loved you. You did it all under the radar and incognito. We respect that. You weren't on that "A-Rod clip Madonna, get some press, send pictures back home to show off to your boys" fame shit. You're a gentleman. Well raised by good parents in Kalamazoo, Michigan, dreaming of a better life in the big leagues, and hoping one day to put up Hall of Fame stats on and off the field. Well, you did it, Derek. You did it big. I know people, Derek. I'm from New York. It's my town. I hear shit. I'm in the streets. I don't read rag magazines or get my info from TMZ, I hear shit they talk about in the pizza spots and the back-alley entrances to nightclubs and shit. Yeah, I don't really club a lot because of my knees and age and whatever, but you get where I'm coming from. I know about you. I like it all. And you had the ability to keep high-profile chicks low. That's a great gift that's not talked about much. You had the skill of a World-Class Stickman.

You handled Mariah Carey like she never even had a song out. You know how tough that is? You had her on lock like you went to high school with her. She's out there now in the news taking dudes' money just for dating them, and you had that on platinum-selling silence! That's real stickman shit right there. And you didn't brag or put women on your arm to parade everywhere; you did it all like a gentleman. And you didn't judge either, Derek. You had women I wouldn't even call back. Yeah, man. You let your small-town roots bloom and made 'em all feel like they had a shot. Sure, you loafed out with pop stars, actresses, and models, but you, my friend, were not afraid to wind sprint your way into a cleaning lady just to let motherfuckers know you were from Kalamazoo. You didn't come out here and go Hollywood with it; you were a man of the people. And everyone got treated nicely. That's what I like to hear. Rumors were floating around that postcoital women got gift baskets! You bring a woman in, you put on some music, you take out the loaf, make magical things happen, then you hand out T-shirts, hats, and signed hardballs when it's over. That's real shit, Derek. You're a multipurpose Hall of Famer. Thanks for the memories, man. Seriously.

Dominique Wilkins

I know it seems out of left field, but so is this book. Dominique Wilkins was known as the Human Highlight Film both on the floor and in the bedroom. Dominique spent the Eighties and Nineties flying through the air slam dunking on every dime piece in sight. We know, man. The respect was earned, not given. When people still discuss your sexual prowess almost seventeen years after you're out of the league, we know some real shit went down.

There are women in Atlanta in their late forties and early fifties who still have your picture in their living room hanging right next to real family photos. Yeah, it ain't in the bedroom, because no real husband of Atlanta wants to see Nique on their woman's wall. That just upsets other men. I know these things. Please trust me here. I don't name names here, and I never reveal my sources, but let's just say that since my foray into the sporting world, your name has come up many, many times when it comes to fantastic stickmen who handled entire regions. It wasn't just Atlanta—Dominique Wilkins had the entire Southeast on lockdown. You ask anyone who played with, for, or against Dominique Wilkins, and they will tell you: home or away, in a house or in a stadium, a nearby park or a southern garage, even a nightclub or pub, when Nique came through your town, Loafzilla showed its face, and people locked their fucking doors. Yeah, not everyone could come out and play. People put their kids to bed early if Dominique was playing in town. And he kept it scandal free and gentleman heavy, which I must repeat is the sign of a true stickman. Dominique scored a 10 in the dunk contest and a 10 at the after party. That's what he did. So, I don't want to hear shit from any of you new-school dudes on Snapchats and Insta-Dick-Pic. I'm talking about that old-school, old-fashioned shit where you had to have real charisma and charm coming off that visitors' bus after a hard-fought game in Utah. Miss your style, man.

Jack Nicholson

We don't have this chapter without talking about Jack Nicholson. The Joker's game was no joke. Jack's stickman status was solidified in the late Sixties and throughout the Seventies, and the streets are still fucking reeling. Right now, at age eighty, Jack keeps four girls in the second row at every Laker game who are there to possibly join him for a late-night milkshake and a swim just for old times' sake.

Jack is a legend. And yeah, could I have researched even older-school legends and gone over what was happening in the days of Sir Laurence Olivier and Clark Gable, of course, but why the fuck would I do that? I'm not writing a history book here, I'm making a list. And Jack Nicholson's mythology was building at a time we still hear about to this day. A time when the Playboy Mansion was going off, and Hollywood free-your-mind sexcapades were going down like never before.

Jack was unfolding the loaf at the Mansion next to the monkey cage, and no one was saying shit. He had the grotto on lock, and they brought him hors d'oeuvres. He had Ms. June and Ms. July arguing over who would see his infamous "Shining Stick" first in the game room, all while Hugh Hefner in his prime was rocking the silk robe and watching *Easy Rider* in the movie room just to make Jack think he was cool. And I personally don't think it's over. Jack's in his eighties and handling the game like a professional gentleman. And this is on some pure charm shit, too. Let's face it, Jack's not the best-looking leading man of all time. He's not walking around with Clooney's bone structure or Channing Tatum's shoulders. He don't give a fuck. He's Jack, and that's what separates the greats from the pack.

To raise your stick game to nearly the same heights as your acting game? That's amazing, not to mention exhausting. I'm tired just thinking about how late into the deep, dark nights Jack was going. And once again, like many a man before him, Nicholson was doing it pre-internet. There was no members' dating apps making shit easy back then; this was straight-up, indoor, low-pro, true-to-the-art-form stick game. You'll never see any cock shots from the Joker. He didn't need them. This was when cocaine and pool parties were happening on Monday mornings. This ain't no Justin Bieber, ass-naked-on-a-yacht shit. Jack didn't need a yacht. He just needed a room. He and his crew were on some "show up at the party, walk in, no one talk, pick out the most beautiful woman, find the white horse, and handle your business" shit. This was the heyday of the sexual revolution. And Jack played it low-key and subtle. He dated Kelly LeBrock, all right? This is public knowledge. I'm not dropping any inside narc shit! Yo, Kelly LeBrock was so fine that they made a movie about the perfect woman built by geeks, and she played her. Jack was getting fictional robot pussy before Austin Powers ever hit the theater circuit. Those were the days. I'm sure there were many nights when he and my man Burgess Meredith just nodded at each other from across the room in the Playboy Mansion.

Wilt Chamberlain

They called him "the Stilt." Obvious or not, he's here. No first-ballot Hall of Fame stickman has had his conquests so openly disputed, discussed, or scrutinized as the Big Dipper. Despite it all, his scoring records on and off the court have yet to be broken, and he stood by his claims until the day he died. The number is twenty thousand. The man vehemently stood by the number of twenty thousand sexual encounters.

Twenty thousand women in his lifetime, and, you know what, not one of them was married. This is 100 percent rumor and not fact checked, but it was from Mr. Chamberlain's mouth, and he stuck by that story. I have no reason to not believe him, and it's too late to ask. Now, look, I don't even know if there are twenty thousand unmarried women on the planet, but he says there were. The man had over 31,000 points, and the infamous 100-point game, and averaged 50 points a game one season, all while laying some mean pipe across the United States of America. One misconception about Wilt was that he bragged about his fuck game. He never bragged about his personal conquests. People were asking him, and he just answered honestly like a gentleman. He wasn't trying to prove anything. He was just "putting it out there for the people who were curious." Yeah, Wilt, guess what, man: we were all fucking curious. I had my guy Ira do the math because I don't have that kind of time, and here's what he came up with. You would've had to have slept with five hundred women a year for forty years straight to put up those numbers. You had to have a few years of 750-plus to even make it happen, Wilt. Either way, I have to give it to you, my man. You did what you did, and the women never came back to sue or complain. They just remembered a good time with a good man and a great athlete. They're raising their kids, and they're keeping their secrets. They don't make them like the Stilt anymore. Rest in peace, Big Fella. You had to be exhausted.

Albert Einstein

Albert Einstein is better known to some as Albert Einstick. Listen up, all you four-eyed, nerdy A students out there: your hero was also a great stickman. Married twice with at least six girlfriends during his second marriage, Big Al was working on the Theory of Pimping before he ever thought about the Theory of Relativity. He figured out long geometry during marathon threesomes. His brain and his loaf searched for answers to the world's toughest scientific questions and found them in a bed with strangers. Einstein made a straight-up list of do's and don'ts for his first wife, including she would cook, clean, and feed him with no guarantee he would return any romantic feelings, and then he made out with his cousin in public. While his brain was hyperevolved, his sex drive was in the animal kingdom. I don't condone marrying your cousin or cheating on your wife while living with a gang of mistresses, but I'll be damned if I'm not putting this legend right where he belongs. He deserves some slack. The guy was stressed the fuck out. You try figuring out Mass Energy Equivalence, the Theory of Relativity, and the random movement of particles and see if you don't need an outlet to release some anxiety from your brain. RIP, Mr. Einsticker; your work and legacy still live on.

Leo

I'd be doing a disservice to this masterpiece of a book if I didn't mention the "Master Piece." This should not come as a shock to you at all if you're living on planet Earth. I'm talking about the one and only "I'm the king of the world and I slept inside the body of a dead horse and fought a bear because the role called for it, then took home the Academy Award while at the same time saving the fucking planet from global warming" Leonardo Mother-fucking DiCaprio. Yeah, this list ends with my man Leo. And once again, I have to say this is not strictly a numbers thing. This is a quality, quantity, privacy, modesty, and non-braggadocious all-multicultural extravaganza. This is a real-life nightclub athleticism, supermodel mixtape. Beloved by men, women, and children, Leo D is alone at the top of the list. Do you have any idea how cool, calm, and classy you have to be to do that many movies and to be on that many sets around that many people at all times and have no one ever, like never, ever say a bad word about you? You would be hard-pressed to find anybody to say anything bad about Leonardo DiCaprio. Leo takes home the gold, hands-down. He's never taken a photograph with anyone under a ten. This is a man who shows up with the most beautiful women on the planet Earth, then takes a picture in a diner where he's eating chicken noodle soup with his mother and his aunt. There is no one better with this. Leo doesn't play games. I don't want to go down the list of names and heights of the women he's dated. That's not the point of this at all. The point is that when it comes to the greatest stickman by pure definition, Leonardo is our number one guy. He loves his mother, he loves his father, he loves the planet, he loves the ladies, and they love him even more. Leonardo, my friend, you have made the impossible possible. Now, get back out there, throw on that grungy baseball hat, cool off the planet a few more degrees, keep doing your thing on and off the silver screen, and tell all the rest of these wannabe Stickmen Bozo the Clowns to shut it down, go home, put in a DVD of *Romeo + Juliet*, and get the fuck away, because the King of Kings is here to stay, and he's a man of the people.

ALL-REGION HONORABLE MENTION STICKMEN STICKLIST

Matt Dillon

Matt Dillon had the Eighties and Nineties on lockdown. My man had a pack of smokes rolled up in his six-dollar T-shirt and took down all the finest pieces in NYC while he was dressed like a gas-station attendant. Girls were giving it up to Matt to get back at their parents. Matt Dillon was an original bad boy. My man had his eighteenth birthday at Studio 54. You had David Bowie in one corner with Mick Jagger and a gang of millionaires in makeup, and eighteen-year-old Matt Dillon and a band of mechanics in another corner. I heard there was one year where he only had sex standing up—no shit. And please don't tell me how well Rob Lowe was doing in the Eighties, okay? I get it. Rob Lowe did his thing, I know. I was there. I saw things I didn't need to see. But Matt Dillon made the burnout in all of us know what was possible if we put our minds to it. I almost started smoking because of him, and I'm still thinking about it.

The Guy Who Clipped Anna Nicole Smith When He Was One Hundred

J. Howard Marshall II is an icon. I have to give him props. I have to. I don't care what the hell was going on with his unit. Maybe it didn't work, maybe it did. Maybe it looked like a sleeping Walter Matthau by the time it was all over. That's not my business. I'm not a doctor. All I know is that this beautiful woman was on TV crying over him and really loved him, and to me, if you're eighty years older than your girl and she's crying on national TV over you, you're doing something right. So, his loaf gets a major shout-out. RIP, Anna Nicole.

Milton Berle

Yeah, I know it's a throwback and may feel random, but don't get it twisted. The Leading Ladies of the Borscht Belt could barely walk after a week with Uncle Milty up in the Catskills. Milton was an anomaly, Jewish yet hung like an Italian sausage. Berle was the first to mix jokes and pokes, and the shit got serious. He bedded Marlene Dietrich and then shocked the Hollywood playboy circuit when he quietly joked his way into Marilyn Monroe's happy place. That's right, folks. Milton even went joke for joke and poke for poke with the great Lucille Ball, too. Not to hurt your eyes, but rumor has it he also gave the magical piece to Nancy Reagan in her heyday. That's as real as it gets. If you look at Berle during the infamous comedy roasts of the Seventies, you'll see the panel flinching every time he walked by on his way to the podium so they didn't get clipped by the baby arm dangling from his region. Uncle Milton was a low-pro legend. From the age of twelve he was performing in Off-Broadway shows, and by the time his pubic hair grew, the no-joke, slow-poke machine was a certified King of the Kosher Salami. I know it's a rough visual, since most of you know Milton as an older man smoking a cigar, but the facts are the facts, and I'd be doing a disservice to the stickman industry if I didn't bring him up.

JFK

For Marilyn Monroe alone you're on the list, bro. Period. You handled the finest piece of ass in all the world, and you did it while in office and let her in and out through the back door like it was your parents' house. Did the loaf get you in trouble a few times? Did people disappear because of the things your loaf did? Did the FBI start Loafgate? Yes, to all of those things. But the bottom line is you're one of the great stickmen of all time. Clinton doesn't move you out of position either. No president does. You swam naked in the White House, and you ran girls out the back on some real rebel-in-the-neighborhood shit. You're in.

JFK Jr.

Sometimes genetics plays a role in how you do with the ladies, and nowhere is it more apparent than with JFK Jr. From '86 to '93, JFK Jr. didn't wear shirts. I personally saw him three times in Central Park riding his bike and felt uncomfortable when he rode by with his chiseled shoulders and hair made of black gold. He took down Daryl Hannah still wet from the mermaid movie, Cindy Crawford in her heyday, and went with true talent when he landed Sarah Jessica Parker in between Broadway gigs, then laid the political loaf down on Brooke Shields when she was still searching for colleges. He took down Madonna in a quick affair that had Jackie O unimpressed and confused, but like father, like son; the stickman never fell far from the tree. Junior was gone too soon in a plane wreck, but the streets are still talking and the legacy lives on. RIP, Junior.

My Boy Vince from Middle School

Vince was skinny as shit and came to school one day in eighth grade and said he had slept with his uncle's girlfriend. I didn't know what that meant, but to me he was a hero and a genuine stickman. Plus, he carried a cane and wore a fedora in high school.

Sinatra

It's no secret that the Chairman of the Board was also the Chairman of the Bedroom. Old Blue Eyes is what they called him. The man needs no introduction. His loaf could've had its own musical career. It should have. It probably would have gone platinum. Who the hell knows what it would have sung about. I don't give a shit. Put out a *Loaf's Greatest Hits* and we're listening. Sinatra is on the list for everything under the stickman umbrella.

Madonna

Yeah, I know she's a woman, but guess what: she was taking young dudes off the streets and giving them hope for the future. Madonna was a great stickman because she was twenty years older than all the dudes she dated in the last ten years, and that makes her a legend and a hope provider for the youth of today, who need it more than ever. I love Madonna, and she's still going strong.

John Mayer

As soon as "Your Body Is a Wonderland" hit the airwaves, his magic stick came off the tour bus, and panties dropped into the garbage. Forget the Katy Perrys and Jennifer Anistons. Do you have any idea the number of common street beauties from Kentucky to Rhode Island that got to take long walks after hearing Mayer perform? Mayer's finger picking was used as a subconscious seduction method last seen from the great Chuck Berry. Mayer could have easily been up there in the main section of the chapter, but his face is too clean and his songs are too soft to make it into the true animal section. His hit single "Daughters" had to come with parental guidance warnings, and there's not even a curse word in it. Women were seen listening to it and having "sleepwalking"-type symptoms, only they were walking in his hotel lobby and not listening to security when asked to leave. Mayer's loaf belongs out there with that of the Mick Jaggers and Robert Plants of the world.

Ed Sheeran

Not only is my man single-handedly responsible for the rise of the ginger man's ability to get busy, but he's doing it all while riding a fucking beach cruiser. Sheeran looks half homeless and fresh out of high school, yet he's putting up staggering street numbers and needs to be recognized. Turning down famously hot ass and saying no to prime-time snapper in exchange for writing time and song crafting, this redheaded gnome who could give a fuck about his hair goes down in our honorable mention section without hesitation. God bless him, we should all be so confident regardless of looks, dress, skin tone, or genetics. Give a man a guitar and a hit song, and it doesn't matter if he looks like he walked out from under a bridge to get some food and then went back to bed in a sleeping bag. Redheads rise up!

Warren Beatty

Beatty didn't make the "Greatest of All Time" list because it's too obvious, and the stories are too well documented at this point. But for all you younger readers who may think of Warren Beatty only as the guy who fucked up the Best Picture announcement of 2017, learn your history. Mr. Beatty was once the King of La

La Land. He was Mr. Moonlight. He is commonly referred to as the Stickman's Stickman. They called him Mr. Wonderful.

He set the bar so high, and his records and reputation are so untouchable, that actual studies are still being worked on to comprehend what he accomplished. So, when you see a living legend like this, stand up and salute him and all he did for the Stickman community. His legacy is untouchable and undeniable.

DISHONORABLE DISCHARGE

Alex Rodriguez

A-Rod: Yes, brother, yes. This hurts me more than it hurts you. Every record you broke on the baseball field was most likely done on PEDs, so who's to say the loaf wasn't also on PEDs as well? Viagra, Cialis, or even that Cuban Missile Crisis Dick Drug we've heard so much about. We're aware of your stellar work as a cocksman; we're not denying the general accomplishments. Congrats. You brought Kate Hudson out of her good-family comfort zone, bringing Goldie and Kurt to games looking like two parents scared of their daughter's new boyfriend. You clipped Cameron Diaz fresh off the silver screen, and we all watched Madonna show up at the stadium and act like she loved baseball. But we can't put you in the mix, bro. It remains to be seen if the PEDs keep you out of the Hall in Cooperstown, but they definitely keep you out the Stickman Hall of Fame.

Note: This list is 100 percent unchecked and well documented by nothing. We've done extensive research yet can't confirm the validity of anything on this list. I encourage you to add to this list or create your own.

These Sneakers Are Made for Walking

I used to love a fresh new pair of kicks: Pro-Keds, Chuck Taylors, Ponys, Nike, Adidas, Converse All Stars. When I was rockin' them, I felt strong, and it felt like my game was better. I walked cooler, talked cooler. Sneaker swag was real.

I spent time lacing them up so they looked and felt perfect. Sometimes I had to do it twice because I'd miss a loop on the first go-round and have to go back to the beginning. The whole thing was a ritual. Some people laced over the top and into the loop, giving it that clean crossover look. My homeboy Aaron from Boston taught me the lace-up game where the end of the lace poked into the plastic of the shoe so the ends ballooned out and looked like dangling liberty bells. I started going with the two laces per shoe move and rocked the double-cross color style for a while. It was all about getting your kicks ready to be seen out in the world.

In the Seventies, Pro-Keds and Converse Chuck Taylors were the shit. They had dope colors and were made out of that heavy potato-sack canvas. Everyone my age was wearing them. Eventually they would tear apart, because when we were kids we actually wore the damn shoes out. The rubber sole would straight up peel off, but they were so comfortable that you didn't even want a new pair. You'd just be walking around with a floppy sole until you pulled the sneaker apart, dissected it to the guts, and started all over with a new pair.

I got my first pair of dope leather sneakers for our yearly Hanukah Christmas Confusion in the City Rapaport Family Gathering. They were the Puma Clydes, the first signature sneaker ever made. They were a huge deal in New York because Walt Frazier was our guy. They were white with the black Puma stripes, and I loved the way they looked regardless of the fact that my feet killed me when I wore them. I realized later it was because they had no arch support, and for me at a young age, the curse of being a Flat-Footed Jew was a fact I'd have to come to grips with for life. I would wear them all day every day until they peeled off my feet and went to the trash. Like I said, I wore the shit out of them. It's what we did. It's what every kid did. We wore the shoes!

I remember I got some leather Converse All Stars that Doctor J made famous in the Eightes, and though I never found them with the red stripe and star, I rocked them daily with the blue stripe. I would scrub the shoes with a paper towel and a toothbrush to freshen them up before I took to the streets. I had two pairs at the same time, so I would wear one for everyday use and the other for basketball until sooner or later both wound up raggedy. The Sneaker World was getting to all of us, and we loved it. But we loved it because we couldn't wait to wear them, to show them off at school or at the park. And when it was time to say good-bye, we let them go. We didn't save our shoes for the closet or keep them around to sell later or put them on the wall like a picture—hell to the no. We got the sneakers because we needed the damn sneakers and wanted the freshest shit out there.

Today, that's no longer the case. I don't know what the fuck is going on, and I can't pinpoint the tipping point, but kids are buying shoes to NOT WEAR them. They're actually begging their parents for some shoes they don't want to wear. This shit doesn't make any sense.

Maybe it was the Air Jordans that sparked Sneaker Culture, but even when those hit the shelves, it was about showing them off on your feet. Yes, I know there were kids getting beaten up for them and, yes, there were fights in the streets and in schoolyards over them, but those were just a few bad apples, and it was all because they were jealous. The point is, your shoes are made for walking, for running, and for being on your damn feet, not for keeping in the box and telling your friends about them.

Back in the day, you wore your Jordans out until they were beat up, dirty, muddy, and ripped apart. Then you threw them in the trash or saved them for a rainy day or a snowstorm. Put your damn shoes on, kids! Are you going to sell them on the market for a few dollars more than you bought them? No, you're going to sell them on the market for a few dollars more than your parents paid when they bought them for you.

Speaking of parents buying sneakers for their kids: my son once dragged me through New York City looking for a pair of Converse Comme des Garçons for his twelfth-birthday present. I didn't know what the shoes were. I thought we were going to Foot Locker, and he looked at me like I was a stranger. "Dad, Foot Locker doesn't carry the Garçons, you know that." I know that? I can't even pronounce that shit. My son pulled me into five different hipster boutiques before we found the shoe. They were cool looking, don't get me wrong, but shit wasn't functional! They had giant red bug eyes painted on the sides, but the soles looked like you shouldn't even walk fast in them. Of course I bought them for him, and the shoe looks great sitting on his end table and in the selfie photo my son took of himself holding the shoes. And I'm out a few hundred bucks and confused as to how he got one over on me. But that's what they do now: they buy shoes to never wear 'em.

They don't wear them outside, inside, on the court, or in life. The damn shoes sit in the box like they're in a shoe coffin. Sneakers are made to be worn. Get them out of the box and take them outside and see what it feels like to be fresh and get a compliment, or to feel what it is to go out and play on those new soles before they turn to shit.

No offense to sneaker designers, but shoes are not meant to be works of art. I know there are plenty of gifted and hardworking people making sneakers, but no one named Picasso or Basquiat is on the assembly line. Sorry. I know there's a market out there for high-end sneakers; I'm not blind. I see what's going on with the battle for them bullshit Yeezy Boosts and the Jordan 1s and the Nike Cortez Phase everyone is back on, but let's get real: You're lined the fuck up like sheep, sleeping outside a shoe store with a blanket and a cell phone waiting for a shoe you're never going to wear? Yeezys don't even have a purpose. They're not made for hoops, walking, or running. They might not even be made for rapping in. What I do know is that you need to get back to wearing your sneakers and stop acting like you're collecting dug-up diamonds.

Me and Ali

Muhammad Ali has been a part of my life for as long as I can remember, thanks to a photo that my father was lucky enough to take with the Champ. It's a Rapaport fable for the ages.

My father was working in radio sales in New York and got invited to watch Ali work out in the bowels of the Garden. Ali was there training to fight Frazier for what would become the Fight of the Century.

My dad was a huge fan and couldn't believe his luck that he got to watch Ali skip rope, shadowbox, talk smack, and work the heavy bag in a room full of reporters and celebrities. Everyone was in awe. No one had ever seen an athlete that size with the grace, speed, power, and footwork Ali had. My dad said that after the workout Ali held court like a comedian in the center of the ring. He poked fun at celebrities, taunted reporters, shook hands, and kissed babies. No one broke up a room like Ali. He was Don Rickles with a knockout punch. As Ali headed to the locker room, he passed my father, and my father found his moment. My dad's friend had a camera and he asked Ali to pose for one shot, and he graciously agreed. That photo solidified the bond my father had with the Champ.

The picture became a huge part of our family. And I thought it would be a good idea at age five to take it to school for show-and-tell. My kindergarten was right across the street from our apartment on Seventy-Seventh and York. It was literally twenty-five yards away from our building. Being that close to home in high school would not have been ideal, but in kindergarten it was fine. When I told my dad that I wanted to take the picture to school, he was hesitant but agreed, since it was so close to home and the odds of me losing it were slim. But he said that it was his only picture of him and Ali, and if I lost it, I'd be living in a cardboard box outside. He was dead serious.

He had lost the only picture he had with Rocky Marciano and was not going through that again. It took a lot out of him to tell people he met Rocky Marciano when he had no proof. I know he met Marciano because he told me nine times a year. He loved to put a good story on repeat. Let me be clear: My father is *almost* a great storyteller. His desire to tell stories never matches the actual story. He starts off strong: the topics are gripping, the time period is interesting, and the characters are dynamic, but when it comes to the delivery, he just misses the mark. But the Ali picture was sacred, and I was not going to lose it.

On the day of show-and-tell, I double wrapped the photo in tin foil, smoothed out the surface, and gave a little extra room on both ends of the picture in case, God forbid, I dropped it. I put it inside a plastic zip lock bag, stuffed it under my arm, and rolled out. I mapped out my walk to school that day and my strategy.

I factored in the direction of the wind, which corner would have the least amount of kids while crossing, and what door I was going to enter through once I got there. I'll never forget the walk over. I slowly stepped all twenty-five yards while cradling the photo under my arm like a running back scared to fumble on the one-yard line. I looked both ways before crossing and got there safe and sound with the picture intact. It was go time.

Most kids brought the usual show-and-tell bullshit: their favorite blankets, a crayon set with half the crayons missing, a Matchbox car, or some weird tool from their dad's toolbox. One kid, Eddie, whose parents must have said "fuck hygiene," brought in a white bunny rabbit with pink eyes. The rabbit didn't move, though. When Eddie put the carrot in front of it, the rabbit just stared at it like he was taunting Eddie for bringing him in. The whole time this debacle was happening, I was thinking, Wait till they see the picture of my father and the most famous person on the planet.

Then they called my name.

I strutted to the front of the class and unwrapped my pride and joy one corner at a time. I put the picture on the easel and told the class my version of my father's story. I was hyped, and I started in. For some reason, when I looked up at the class, no one seemed to give a shit except for Eddie, whose rabbit had just shit pellets all over the cage. He was looking at me, but the rest of the class stared at the shit cage. I didn't care. I told that story with every fiber of my body. I was animated and all over the place. You would have thought it was a picture of Ali and me. I recapped the story of my dad meeting the Champ and finally got a few of the kids to listen, even though most were still taunting Eddie's sick rabbit. I gave that performance my all, and when I was finished, I was exhausted. Fuck that bunny for trying to steal my limelight. I'm sure that pebble-shitting rabbit is dead and gone by now, but I still have this picture.

My father, Disco David Rapaport, and Muhammad Ali in the basement of Madison Square Garden, 1971.

The Champ

Muhammad Ali remains a thread that connects me and my father and my brother. We reminisce about the Champ and his fights to this day.

Some of my favorite memories are of sitting in the living room watching Ali and Cosell do their thing on ABC's *Wide World of Sports*. Cosell would talk to Ali, and my dad would be laughing hysterically at their banter. They were like Abbot and Costello. You could sense the love and respect they had for each other. To this day, there's never been an announcer-athlete camaraderie that can touch theirs. Cosell would ask a question, Ali would say something about Howard's hair, and they would just go at it. Keep in mind that this was before the fight, too. How the hell did Ali stay that loose when he was about to get in the ring with a man whose goal was to take his head off? My father would be cracking up watching and tell us, "I love Ali, he's so much smarter than all these other loudmouths. Cosell can't even keep up with him." My father wasn't that into Howard, but I thought he was cool, original hairpiece and all.

We would watch an Ali fight, then talk all night about it. My dad knew boxing, so he would school us on the sport. He would talk about Ali's speed and footwork and how his ability to take a punch would ruin him later in life, and he was right. My dad would break down his fights with Earnie Shavers and Ken Norton and be in awe at the size of the guys Ali was beating. But it was when Ali beat Foreman that the Rapaports realized he was the greatest of all time. The way Ali played possum in that fight and then knocked George out cold on his feet and watched him fall to the ground like a tree in the forest was epic. Of course, you can't talk about Ali if you don't mention Frazier. Those fights were brutal and life changing for both fighters. When I watch that first fight with Frazier when Ali lost, it still upsets me to this day.

Ali got knocked off his feet in the eleventh round by that now-famous leaping left hook. When he hit the canvas, it was like watching your favorite superhero get beat by a villain. Maybe it was the connection my father and I had over Ali. Regardless, it's one of those fights I still have a hard time watching but an even tougher time turning off.

They would fight two more times, and the fights were epic. So were the press conferences.

At the second press conference, Ali and Frazier started fighting live on TV dressed in three-piece suits, and it freaked me out.

Ali got in Joe's face, and Joe, trying to defend himself, got up, and Ali said, "SET down, Joe, SET down." I knew he meant "sit," but with his Louisiana accent it came out "set." I didn't know why Ali and Frazier hated each other, but I took Ali's side. It wasn't until much later in life that I realized their issues went much deeper than just two fighters wanting to take each other's heads off. I was acting like the press conference fight was the real fight.

I started crying, and my father said, "Calm down, Michael, they're not fighting." I told him, "Yes, they are, Dad, and Frazier is a jawbreaker." My brother Eric yelled, "This is fake, dumbass. You're really dumb, Michael," but I was crying, and my dad, standing there wearing his sole pair of black bikini underwear that were way too small, said, "Michael, calm down. They're not fighting. Frazier didn't hit him." My brother screamed, "He didn't hit him. Calm down, loser." And then he smacked me in the back of the head, and I started crying harder. My father then smacked my brother in the back of the head, and he started crying. The whole thing caused chaos in my home.

When Muhammad announced he was coming back in 1980 to fight Larry Holmes, I knew something wasn't right. I received my weekly issue of *Sports Illustrated* with Ali on the cover; he had a mustache and was bloated. My dad, who always grabbed the mail, sadly tossed me my *SI*, knowing how I'd feel when I saw it. Ali's eyes looked glazed over. Something wasn't right.

In the article Ali talked about how he was going to beat Holmes and that Holmes was overrated. Like the rest of the world, I felt secure Ali would win. Why wouldn't he? There's no way Ali doesn't win against a guy I've never heard of, a guy my father never mentioned. Looking back on it, my dad didn't want to bring up the truth: Ali was past his prime, and Holmes had one of the greatest jabs the game had ever seen. Ali was done, but people were still willing to pay to see him. And most of them would regret it.

My father and I watched the fight on Pay-Per-View at Radio City Music Hall. The place was packed. It was weird being at Radio City for a fight, since it was known for everything but boxing. It was home to Sinatra, B. B. King, and the Rockettes.

Not the usual setting for a fight crowd, but the place was sold out. People couldn't wait to see the return of Ali. The only thing I can compare it to is a Mike Tyson fight. The energy was palpable. The entire world craved time with Ali, and they were about to get it.

But the fight was a tragedy. My dad saw it unfolding immediately. "Ali looks slow, Michael. This isn't going to be good." Ali came out slow-footed, glassy-eyed, and heavier than he'd ever been. He was a shell of everything we knew, but I still had hope. "Come on, Champ, play possum for as long as you want, but when he drops that jab, come over the top with the big right and drop him like you did Foreman. You can do it, Champ, let's go." But it was not to be that night. Things got so bad that Larry Holmes himself actually asked the ref to stop the fight. There can be no worse feeling than to nearly kill your hero in the ring.

At one point my father was yelling at the screen, "Stop the damn fight!" He wanted to leap through the screen. The fight was finally stopped when Angelo Dundee made Ali call it quits. I was crushed. My dad had to pull me up from my seat and walk me out of the theater.

After the fight, I rode home on the back of my father's BMW motorcycle. As we drove back home, I cried the entire way and wiped my tears and snot on the back of my father's coat. It was a sad night for everyone.

The Champ Makes Grown Men Cry

Years later I met Ali. It was 1997 at the Independent Spirit Awards.

I was there with my friend actor Kevin Corrigan, whom I'd met while filming *Zebrahead*. You may know Kevin's work more than his name. Kevin's a great talent, and that year the Spirit Awards nominated him for best supporting actor for his role in *Walking and Talking*. My man Benecio del Toro ended up winning the award, but I love him, too, so it was all good.

The Spirit Awards are like the Oscars for indies. There's something beautiful about the indie world of moviemaking. People make films with passion, blood, sweat, and tears. To make an indie, you have to give it everything. This was a great time for independent film, a time when top talent got involved. I remember seeing Sean Penn and John Turturro sitting side by side that night, two of my favorites.

It was a cool event held on the beach in Santa Monica under a giant tent. They gave out gift bags with Sony Discman CD players and gift certificates for massages. Muhammad Ali's documentary *When We Were Kings* was up for an award, and people kept saying the Champ was in the building. Once I heard he was there, I knew I had to meet him. Corrigan and I were scouring the area looking for Ali. I was excited to see him but at the same time I was freaked out. My heart was literally racing. We started looking all over the place for a huge crowd surrounding him but couldn't find it. I saw a security guard and asked, "Is Muhammad Ali really here?" He pointed and said, "Yeah, he's right over there at the table." Holy shit. I looked at Kevin and he looked at me, and, knowing my admiration for the Champ, he wasn't shocked when I beelined it to Ali. I didn't even look back to see if Kevin was with me. My heart was pounding for real. As I got closer, I saw a couple of fans lined up around him saying hello, and there he was, sitting at a table, Muhammad Ali. I really couldn't believe it. He was right there. I recognized his wife, Lonnie, sitting to his left, and his lifelong friend and photographer Howard Bingham to his right. I was a few feet away now and slowly moving in. A couple of people said hello to me, but I could only focus on Ali. I stood behind the other fans who were reaching down to shake his hand . . . and then I was up.

Here I was about to shake the hand of my hero. He was a man I considered a great friend, yet we'd never met. I got to the Champ and shook his right hand, which was shaking lightly from the Parkinson's that had taken over his body, and I leaned down just a little bit and said, "Champ, you have meant so much to me for my entire life, and it's a such an honor to meet you." I stood up, ready to move on, but couldn't budge. I literally couldn't move. I leaned back down right next to his ear, and without thinking, I whispered, "I know you're okay, Champ. I know you're doing okay and I love you," and then I stood straight up. God and Kevin Corrigan as my witness, Ali quickly looked me in the eyes and motioned with one finger for me to lean down again. I leaned down right next to him. I thought the Champ was going to say something, but he kissed me right on the cheek. I couldn't believe it. I started crying, literally sobbing, and wrapped my arms around him as though he just saved my life. I said, "I love you so much, I love you so much, Muhammad." At this point I was out of my body and tripping out for real. I kissed his right hand, and I remember noticing at that very moment that his hands were huge but also incredibly soft for a man who had used them to give out so many beatings. I finally stood up, and I was still crying and I wasn't sure why. I know I wasn't crying because I felt bad for Muhammad Ali. I think I cried because I literally loved him so much. I also wanted him to know that I knew he was "okay." I have always heard him say in the press that he didn't want people to feel sorry for him because of what the Parkinson's disease had done to him. He always made it clear that he was happy and he felt like he had a blessed life. I hadn't expected to get so emotional when I met him; it just happened.

The Greatest of All Time passed away on June 3, 2016, and

not a day goes by that I don't think about him, and I only met him that one time. I recently read an article in which Lonnie Ali talked about how common it was for people to have an emotional reaction to meeting Muhammad. It happened to me right then and there, and it's something I will never forget.

The Skinny-Jeanification of Sports

SKINNY-JEANIFICATION: (*noun*) the softening of athletes due to the "look at me" culture that's been growing in sports as a result of the "selfie" generation's desire to promote themselves before bettering themselves.

The Skinny-Jeanification of sports has taken over, and it's a major concern—not only of mine but of some of my favorite fellow ranters. I recently saw Jalen Rose hang his head after seeing what athletes were wearing at their postgame press conferences. As Jalen Rose and others have noted, the problem is bigger than just the dress codes and fashion. The Skinny-Jeanification is some real monumental bitch shit.

Now, there's a misconception that Skinny-Jeanification is solely about athletes showing up to games or press conferences looking like they're ready for a Gucci runway show in Paris. This is not entirely true. Yes, Skinny-Jeanification was sparked by the new fashion styles of people like Cam Newton, who showed up for games and interviews dressed like a member of a Sockless Barbershop Quartet or Pinocchio's giant twin brother in a bow tie and bright mismatched colors, or Dwayne Wade, who looked like a mannequin that got robbed before he made it to the display window at Macy's men's store in Manhattan. I love you, D-Wade, but burn that short-sleeve blazer you so proudly wear, and let's act like it never happened.

Odell Beckham's search for the perfect shade of magenta hair had us all fucked up and only made things worse. When Odell was voted top five best dressed at the 2016 Met Gala, and numbers one through four were Rihanna, Katy Perry, Beyoncé, and a Thai male supermodel without a name, the fashion world thought they had a new god—a gold-tipped, ball-catching, superathletic fashion god. Well, they didn't. Even my main man Russell Westbrook, the single-season triple-double record holder, is out of control. Yo, Russ, you're rolling around like every day is Halloween. This season alone he was the Little Drummer Boy one day, followed by looking like Pat Benatar on her "Hit Me with Your Best Shot" tour, and then strolled into an afternoon game looking like Fabio had fucked Kurt Cobain, and no one had the balls to say shit. Well, I do, because I can't help it. Westbrook is wearing a piece inspired by the movie *Black Swan*, and no one's batting an eye? Fuck it, go ahead and break out your *Pirates of the Caribbean* gear, Russ, and call it a day, because there's no turning back now. Rock the mask from *Eyes Wide Shut* if you're feeling it. Listen, like I said, this ain't just about the outfits, and I'm not a fashion icon. If you YouTube me, you'll see me on three talk shows wearing the same shirt on every one of them, and they were all shot in the same week. I'm aware of my limitations when it comes to fashion. I dress strictly for comfort, recognition, and price point; fuck it. But like I said, the dress code is just a symptom of an entirely bigger problem.

So, allow me to quote the great Keith Sweat here when I say, "Something just ain't right." Skinny-Jeanification represents the softening of the entire sports world, and it could bleed into the youth of today if we don't nip it in the bud. Skinny-Jeanification is a side note and an offshoot of the Me Generation steeped in selfies and self-promotion and "Hey, guys, look at how interesting I am while I'm showing you my BRAND." I get it. Branding is part of the world we live in now. It's an overused fucking word that has every athlete in the world thinking they're so damn original that they can build a business around their unique BRAND. Well, guess what the best brands are made of? Great fucking products. Yeah, the brand needs to be good before it can be sold, my man. These guys are thinking about their brand before thinking about getting a championship. You're thinking about your branding and marketing when you need to be thinking about your defense and your off-season workouts. How the hell are you going to build a brand when you're just average? Of course, there are a few exceptions—there always are. LeBron James can show up in a fishnet half shirt with a mermaid tail and eyeliner and it's absolutely fine. Why? Because he's got the personal statistics, team statistics, and the championship rings to prove it. But some of you dudes are missing the point, and you're spending an hour cropping your selfie when that hour should have been spent figuring out how the fuck you're going to stop Kyrie from going left on you every time. You know what would look great with your Manolo Blahnik shoes and your Comme des Garçons silk shirt in your heavily filtered selfie from the yacht of a billionaire you never met? A fucking championship RING.

The Selfie Generation wants to be like Mike, but it doesn't want to work like Mike. Mike wasn't trying to dress like a nine-year-old Japanese girl to promote his brand. Mike didn't dress for shit because he was too busy staying after practice shooting free throws for five hours. Mike didn't take pictures of himself because he was working on his defensive footwork to stop Magic and attempt to keep Larry Bird from busting his ass the next week.

Mike didn't have time to pick out an outfit that looked like a Ken doll because he wanted the ring.

These guys are so busy documenting every aspect of every single day that there's no way they can be improving on the court and on the field. I get it—it's a different time in the world. But it's really not. It's still about being great, not about being seen. These motherfuckers grew up watching so many episodes of *Entourage* that they think they're all gonna be Vinny Chase. You ain't the centerpiece of the world, Holmes. A lot of you dudes are gonna wind up as Johnny Drama if you keep snapping selfies and skipping free-throw practice. Wake up.

All Everything superstar Steeler wide receiver Antonio Brown went live postgame on Facebook from the Steelers' locker room with his teammates walking around butt-ass naked. He even recorded tough-as-nails, hard-core, all-business Coach Mike Tomlin giving a postgame speech that should have been private. The speech was amazing, and I was even knocking out sets of push-ups after hearing it, but it wasn't for the public. You're a motherfucking Pittsburgh Steeler, not a fourteen-year-old girl at a One Direction concert. Harry Styles ain't checking for you, AB. Try that shit during the terrible Terry Bradshaw days, and Jack Lambert would have shoved that cell phone so far up your keister you'd be shitting out selfies for a month. How the hell is this behavior okay? Skinny-Jeanification is real, and it's spreading like wildfire. It's making these guys soft and self-centered, and it's even turning them into head cases.

Boston Celtic and supposed tough guy Marcus Smart took himself out of a 2017 NBA playoff game because he said, "I didn't think I was playing well." Are you fucking nuts? Can you imagine John Stockton taking himself out of a playoff game because he thought he was having an off night? You think Pistons bad-boy leader Isiah Thomas would ever remove himself from a game because he just wasn't up for it that day, to leave room for someone else to come in and play for him? Zeke played a Finals game with a broken ankle. Did Moses Malone ever take himself out of a game because he had just thrown away a pass? Hell to the no, to the No No No.

Focus on your game before you focus on your brand. Unless you're coming out with a clothing line called Twelfth Man on the Bench or Almost Made It jeans, you need to shift your focus. You're not all LeBron, Russell Westbrook, D-Wade, or even Ezekiel Elliott, the Dallas Cowboys running back who almost broke Twitter by showing up to the 2016 NFL Draft in a motherfucking button-up shirt tucked under to show off his belly button. But Zeke earned the right to wear whatever he wants going forward after having one of the best rookie seasons ever.

The point is, be great at your job before you're great at social media and dressing yourself. Stay that extra few hours in the gym like the great ones did, and don't Snapchat your every moment doing what you're supposed to be doing—then we can let you slide with the nut huggers, clown shoes, and purple bow ties. Now put your fucking cell phone down and do an extra wind sprint.

The Bachelor of Montana

POSTSCRIPT: Phil Jackson, sitting in a rocking chair on his porch, smoking a cigar, and looking out over his multimillion-dollar Montana ranch, dictated the following letter to the great people of New York and the fans of the Knicks. The song "Old Man" by Neil Young can be heard playing in the background.

"Hey, New York, Phil Jackson here. I felt like I needed to share a few things with you so we didn't part ways on bad terms. Damn it, is that a llama? Hold on. Hey, man, come on, not on the lawn! That thing shits like an elephant. Where the hell did he come from? Just snuck up out of nowhere.

"I have to be honest, I didn't plan on any of that stuff going down the way it did in New York. I never saw it coming. I wanted to win badly when I got there. I was trying to do my job, and next thing I knew there was an owner singing in a mediocre blues band and I was tweeting at my own players, which is not my style. I don't tweet. My grandkids do that crap, not me. I lost it for a minute. Damn, this cigar is good. I love a good cherry finish at the tail end of an inhale. I wasn't myself in New York, man. I was falling asleep at random times. I was beat. But you try being in your seventies and staying awake through all that shit. I had to nap. There were days when I double napped. You ever have a two-nap day in New York City? It doesn't even feel right. There are cars and buses and people making noise. Sirens rushing down the street. Bum fights on the corner. That's how tired I was. I napped through all of that shit and still woke up tired. Hey, mountain lion, get out of here, man, I'm trying to focus! Jesus, that thing looks so calm, but could probably kill me if it was mad. Hope it's in a good mood; I'm not running anywhere. Is this thing even on? Hold up, let me see here . . . all right, it's working.

"New York, let me again say I'm sorry it didn't work out. I love New York and I love its people. But I've got a good life now, and I'm enjoying it. The air is fresh, the people are kind, the mushrooms are medicinal, and the mountain ranges are perfect to wake up to. I'm here in Montana, clearing my head and taking long walks and listening to the birds talk it out among themselves. They've got some beautiful birds out here. These aren't New York City birds. These birds are relaxed, just cruising through the sky nice and easy. Life is peaceful here. Two days ago Doris and Eloise came over from another mountain, and I took out my eleven championship rings while sitting around the table and having some tea, and that felt good. Is that a crane? Holy shit, man, I just saw the biggest damn bird I've ever seen. That thing looked like a flying dragon. I love *Game of Thrones*. Mother Nature doesn't ask you permission for anything out here, it just starts dropping these little jewels in front of you.

"By the way, being single out on the range isn't too bad. I was going to do some online dating after my last big public breakup, but turns out it's not for me. I went on one of those sites, and they asked me what my favorite thing about myself was, and all I could think was, shit—I'm Phil Jackson. I won eleven NBA titles and had an amazing career and life, what the hell else do I need to type in? You want me to put in that I mastered the triangle offense and showed the world a way of playing they'd never seen before? I don't think that would be appropriate. You want me to put down 'I turned two NBA franchises around, and that's almost impossible to do in this league'? Not really my style. Was I going to take out an entire page on playing with legends? No. I don't need to. I'm not going to write down things like 'I've made millions of dollars doing what I love, and I never really have to work again if I don't want to.' I would never write that down. I don't do arrogance. I do peace and humility and cigars. So, needless to say, I'm not online dating, and Doris, from what I hear, has a beautiful sister who loves square dancing, fire pits, and bird watching, and, by gosh, that sounds great to me. All that high-society shit I was dealing with and high-profile relationships I was in, that ain't me. I'm an old jock from North Dakota who loves loose-fit clothing and a home-cooked meal followed by a good cigar and a vape here and there. Though the new vape shit is sort of strong, so I don't take more than one hit of it. That shit will have you staring at your hand for two hours wondering if it's connected to your body.

"Either way, when it's all said and done, I hope you all look back someday and realize there were some other things happenin' in New York that I couldn't control. It wasn't all my fault, I'm telling you. My God, that butterfly is stunning. Is that thing purple dominant? You never see that. Wow. Anyway, there was a ton of shit going on in New York that you could never understand. You try being an avid music lover and having your owner show up at three in the morning in the Village to sing like shit in a blues band that doesn't want him in it, man. It messes your head up. I couldn't focus over there; there were too many damn distractions, and I don't do well with distractions anymore. I'm mellowing out in my old age.

"Listen, you guys, I just don't want to get into all that went wrong; let me just say that I wish it was different, you know. I love that city and I love the game of basketball. It's given me everything I could have ever dreamed of for my entire life. And right at this moment I'm dreaming of some warm biscuits and polishing up those championship rings for fun before I set them back on the mantel where they belong for the neighbors to enjoy. I'm good now, you guys. I think I'll mosey on inside and talk to you later, New York.

"I hope one day we can all get along again, and if we do, great, and if not, well, that's life. Hey, llama, not again, man!"

—Phil

The Greatest Ever Eva!!!!

I've talked an enormous amount of shit in these pages, and I'm sure I've even offended more people than I actually planned to. But this book wouldn't be complete if we didn't wrap it up with the only debate that counts: Who are the Top Five Greatest Athletes of All Time?

This right here is the All-World, All-Comprehensive, Non-Debatable, Undeniable Michael Rapaport Top Five Greatest Athletes of All Time. We've all thought about it and battled with our friends over it, but the debate is finally over. You can take this list, keep it in your pocket, and break it out at parties, picnics, or anytime the topic rears its head. Now, let's do this once and for all.

At the top of my list and holding firm at the number one spot is Serena Williams! I know you're thinking, Rapaport's going outside the box with tennis, and look at how politically correct he's trying to be by choosing a woman as number one. Not true. I understand some of you cretins don't even think tennis is a legit-enough sport to appear on my list. Well, it is. And guess what: it's not about the sport as much as it's about Serena's absolute, 100 percent, ridiculous domination. Twenty-three Grand Slam wins, the last one while she was pregnant, plus twenty-one singles titles, and I don't even need to talk about what she and Venus did to the poor players they beat up in doubles over the years. And let's just be real: when I went on her Wikipedia page, it had so many colors, graphs, and lines for countries and places where she wrecked opponents that I had to get off the page before I had a seizure from staring at it. Serena Williams has a lifetime record of 783–130. Did you hear that? No one in her sport has ever come close. So, coming in at numero uno and not going anywhere is Serena Williams.

Now, number two has me a bit more confused, since there are so many damn athletes and sports. Shit. There's an argument for Tony Hawk or jockey Little Willie Shoemaker, but I don't work like that. On my list, you need balls. You need to throw a ball, hit a ball, dribble a ball, catch a ball, or run with your balls flying to make the list.

So, for my number two—and it irks me to give it up to this guy so early because I really don't like him—I have to say I'm picking Michael Jordan. I hate that I'm giving it up to MJ so early, but I had to do it. Over 32,000 points lifetime, averaged over 30 a game for his entire career, and the jackass's logo is still on everything, everywhere you look around the world. He took home six championships, he was a ten-time NBA scoring champion, the fucking guy never lost in the NBA Finals, and he scored 38 points with the flu and no chicken soup. So yeah, Mike, there ya go. You got the number two spot. Now go tell your friends you made my list.

Hold on, something just hit me. Michael Jordan was a two-sport athlete and wasn't so great at one of them. Hold up. If I'm going to give it up for a two-sport athlete, I'm picking my man Bo "Motherfucking Run You Over Brian Bosworth Whenever I Feel Like

It" Jackson. Sorry, Mike. Yeah, it happened fast. I'm giving my number two to Bo Jackson, and Jordan's down at three and I don't feel bad about it. So, Bo Jackson is coming in at number two. I don't think I really need to hit you with stats on Bo Jackson; we all saw him break baseball bats over his knee. The man won the Heisman in college, ran over everyone in the pros and was a phenom in baseball where he was an all-star and an MVP. If you need to really check out what Bo did, go check his ESPN 30 for 30 and call me. We can talk.

So, we have Serena, Bo, and Michael. I like this list. The list is building nicely. Oh fuck, man, wait—how can I talk two-sport athletes when I forgot about the greatest three-sport athlete? Sorry, kids, I just remembered Handsome Jim Thorpe, arguably the finest athlete to ever live. A three-sport legend who's still being talked about today, even though he was around before treadmills. He played pro football, pro baseball, and won the gold medal in the decathlon in the 1912 Olympics. The guy did everything. And if all this shit is relative, maybe he's number one. No, I can't go number one with Thorpe; sorry, Jimbo. He had the same body then that I have now. I can't give number one to a guy who's built like all my relatives. I'm keeping Serena in her place, even though Thorpe made a comeback in football when he was forty-one. When I was forty-one, I came back to the couch with ice cream and a blanket. I'll put Thorpe at two and move Bo to three, and Jordan—bye-bye three and hello four.

So, we've got Serena Williams, Jim Thorpe, Bo Jackson, and Michael. Shit, man, I'm trying to stay on land sports, but I keep seeing Michael Phelps in my head. Twenty-three gold medals and broke a sixty-eight-year-old record? No, I'm staying on land before I lose control of my own list here. Balls, balls, balls. Yeah, sorry, Phelps, but you'll be okay. Stop doing bong hits and get back on the Wheaties box. Number five is coming in hot. I know a lot of you are thinking Jim Brown, Walter Payton, Caitlyn/Bruce Jenner, or Insane Usain Bolt, but guess who's coming to dinner?

My man Muhammad Ali is coming in hot at number five. I have to do it. I can't see this list being legitimate without Ali. He's the greatest of all time, with the fastest hands ever seen on a heavyweight. There is no tougher sport on the planet, and he made it look effortless. I'm not doing the top five without the Champ. Muhammad, welcome to the list.

So, we've got Serena, Thorpe, Bo, Michael, and Ali. That's one hell of a list. Shit. Hold on, wait a minute. Something just hit me. If we're talking about dominating a sport, I can't go on without mentioning Canadian superhero Wayne Gretzky.

How the hell am I supposed to have a "greatest athletes of all time" list without the Great One?! He set scoring records that will never be touched. Wayne's got 894 regular-season goals alone. He shattered the assist record with 1,963 assists, and half of them were no-look passes. And this white-bread wonder boy with absolutely no lips had 2,857 lifetime points and fifty hat tricks! I could give two shits about hockey, but I think Wayne Gretzky needs to be here. Fuck me!

Every time Great Wayne touched the puck, it went in. He was doing shit on skates no one could do on their feet. Shit, maybe I move Ali down to six, Wayne to five, and keep Jordan at four . . . Fuck that. I'm not moving Ali off this list. No way. I won't do it, Champ. Right now, you're tied at the five spot, and that's where

I'm keeping you. So, we have Serena, Bo, Jordan, Thorpe, Ali, and Wayne. But wait. That's six. Hold up.

Is baseball even a sport to consider a "greatest athlete" coming from, since you're sitting around most of the time? What am I talking about? Sorry, of course it's a real sport. They're running, throwing, hitting that little-ass ball at a hundred miles an hour—yeah, it's real. I might have to throw my road dawg George Herman "Babe" Ruth in there. The guy smoked cigars, stuffed his face with hot dogs and beer, and then went to the plate and knocked the shit out of the ball. He's gotta go on the list. He's Babe Ruth. I know he played when baseball wasn't integrated, but the fact that he did what he did while being a chubby, unhealthy mess is a medical miracle. The guy had 714 home runs without steroids or diet. Now, this is very challenging. Am I sending mixed messages to children by putting a guy built like Santa Claus on the "best of the best" list? I hate to do it, but, Babe, you're coming off. No hard feelings.

Okay, okay, okay, here we go, I have this under control. Bo Jackson, my friend, you're gonna take a little trip up to three. Muhammad Ali, my main man, you'll be okay at four. And I'll give Wayne and MJ a tie at five.

5. Air Jordan and the Great One
4. Ali
3. Bo Jackson
2. Big Jimmy Thorpe
1. Serena

I'm all fucked up. Why does Jim Brown keep popping into my head? You ever see Jim Brown highlights? That was a grown-ass man playing with boys. We gotta get Jim Brown in here. Wait! Was

Bruce Lee an athlete? Why wouldn't he be? Damn it! Leaping up and kicking apples off bad guys' heads is real. What about Pelé? Fuck soccer. Wait. Do I bring LeBron in here? I don't fucking want to bring him in. I'm not feeling that today, LeBron. Sorry, your ring-chasing nonsense is holding you off my list for now. Besides, you're not just skipping past Kobe Bean Bryant on my watch. Is Walter Payton in the house? Who can I take off the list to make room for Sweetness? I'm losing my shit, man.

You know what, folks? I'm sorry, make up your own list—I can't do it. Lists are for groceries. There's no fucking list . . . although, we could go top ten. Michael Rapaport's Top Ten List? You know what, sports lovers? You'll get that in the sequel. I'm fucking spent, and I'm sorry, folks. I'm all ranted out.

Acknowledgments

Mike Young, Mike Young, and Mike Young: Thank you for holding me down and guiding me through this book-writing process. You're the real MVP of *This Book Has Balls*. You're a great writer and a patient man. You kicked ass for me.

Julian and Maceo.

Eric Rapaport: My Big Smarter Brother.

Gerald Moody: My Brownsville, Brooklyn, comrade since 1982.

Everyone in Brownsville, Brooklyn, who held me down in the Eighties and Nineties Howard Projects.

The BRC.

Everybody in Harlem World for accepting me, no questions asked.

The *I Am Rapaport* stereo podcast producers Miles and Jordan.

My Young Shooter, Dean Collins.

Bahr Brown, Jason Bergh, Michelle Lee: My Other Momma, Dean Moody.

Mark Lonow, JoAnne Astrow, and Claudia Rapaport: You gave me my career and so much more. I'll never forget it.

Daniel Greenberg: THANK YOU SO MUCH for the foresight to imagine I had a book in me.

Matthew Benjamin, the real editor of this book: THANK YOU for everything. Sincerely.

My Top Twenty Favorite Athletes Who I Didn't Mention in the Book But Should've.

1. Jack Lambert (I dreamed of being you in '81.)
2. Latrell Sprewell (Needs no explanation.)
3. Kenny Anderson (Best to ever do it.)
4. Le'Veon Bell (My vessel into fantasy football.)
5. Chris Mullin (You deserved a whole chapter for real.)
6. Mark Bavaro
7. Joe Klecko and Mark Gastineau (NY Sack Exchange lives forever.)
8. Reggie Jackson
9. Apollo Creed
10. Sugar Ray Leonard
11. Iran Barkley from the Boogie Down Bronx
12. Shaquille O'Neal
13. Moses Malone
14. Aaron Pryor
15. George "the Iceman" Gervin
16. The Fab Five
17. The Boston Bruins who beat up the fans in Madison Square Garden: you sick fucks, you.
18. Tim Hardaway
19. Mahmoud Abdul Rauf, formerly known as Chris Jackson (Steph Curry before Steph Curry)
20. Isiah Thomas (One of my favorites ever.)

I apologize to the teachers, principals, and students of the ten schools I attended.

Index

About the Author

Michael Rapaport is an actor and director who's appeared on TV shows such as *Friends*, *Justified*, *The War at Home*, and *Prison Break*, and in films such as *True Romance* and *Mighty Aphrodite*. He directed the award-winning 2011 documentary *Beats, Rhymes & Life: The Travels of a Tribe Called Quest* and an ESPN 30 for 30 film, *When the Garden Was Eden*, that premiered in 2014. His *Barstool Sports* podcast, *I Am Rapaport*, has almost two million monthly listeners and regularly makes the iTunes top 50. He's also a diehard Knicks fan. *This Book Has Balls* is his first book.